YORK NOT

General Editors: Professor
of Stirling) & Professor Su
University of Beirut)

Ernest Hemingway

FOR WHOM THE BELL TOLLS

Notes by Stewart Sanderson

MA (EDINBURGH)
Director, Institute of Dialect and Folk Life Studies
University of Leeds

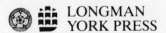 LONGMAN
YORK PRESS

YORK PRESS
Immeuble Esseily, Place Riad Solh, Beirut.

LONGMAN GROUP LIMITED
London
Associated companies, branches and representatives
throughout the world

©Librairie du Liban 1980

First published 1980
ISBN 0 582 78236 8
Printed in Hong Kong by
Sheck Wah Tong Printing Press Ltd

Contents

Part 1: Introduction   *page* 5

Hemingway's life and work   5

A note on the text   13

Part 2: Summaries   14

A general summary   14

Detailed summaries   16

Part 3: Commentary   54

The moral theme   54

Heroes and the code   56

Structure and style   60

Part 4: Hints for study   62

Study files   62

Examination questions   65

Specimen answers   65

Part 5: Suggestions for further reading   69

The author of these notes   70

Part 1

Introduction

Hemingway's life and work

Ernest Hemingway was born in Oak Park, Illinois, on 21 July 1899, and died at his home in Ketchum, Idaho, on 2 July 1961, shortly before his sixty-second birthday.

In these years he had led an extraordinarily active and varied life and had also achieved extraordinary success as a writer. This success is not to be measured in commercial terms alone, though Hemingway made a great deal of money out of his books and the occasional journalism of his middle years. Above all he was successful as a literary artist.

His influence on other writers of fiction, for instance, is widely acknowledged. Critics and reviewers have adopted, as part of their standard frame of reference, phrases such as 'the Hemingway hero' and 'the Hemingway style', referring to aspects of the content and the form of his writing. Finally in 1954 his achievement as an artist was recognised by the award of the Nobel Prize for Literature, special mention being made of his 'powerful style-forming mastery of the art of modern narration'. The Nobel citation also drew attention to the central themes of his work—courage; intellectual and emotional honesty; generosity of spirit; and the author's 'natural admiration of every individual who fights the good fight in a world of reality over-shadowed by violence and death'.

In *For Whom The Bell Tolls* these themes are all richly developed and displayed. First published in 1940, the novel marks a particular climax in Hemingway's explorations of the techniques of fiction. As we shall see, the narrative devices which he uses allow him to range backwards and forwards in time beyond the boundaries of the three days in which the action of the novel takes place, beyond the handful of characters involved in that action, and beyond the Spanish mountain-range which is the geographical setting of the action. This is in striking contrast to his earlier novels and short stories. So too is the prose style, which is more complex, and is organised in fuller periods, than that of his earlier work. After *For Whom The Bell Tolls* he once more moved in new directions, experimenting with constructional and stylistic devices that were different again. This novel therefore occupies a central position in the study of his development as an artist;

and in order to appreciate it fully we must first of all consider it within the total context of his work. And since one of Hemingway's basic theories was that writers should write only of what they truly know, we must also consider those aspects of his life's experience which shaped his work.

Hemingway's family was typical of the middle-class professional and business inhabitants of Oak Park, a prosperous suburban town near Chicago. His grandfather, a Civil War veteran, ran a real estate business; his father practised as a family doctor; his mother was trained as a professional singer and continued to teach music after her marriage. There were six children, Ernest being the second and the elder of the two sons. The parents were very different in temperament. Dr Hemingway was gentle, shy and reserved, a sensitive man who later, when suffering from diabetes and heart disease, took his own life with his father's military revolver. Hemingway's mother was rather domineering, self-righteous, and active in the social affairs of the local church, whereas his father enjoyed solitary outdoor activities. A keen naturalist, he passed this enthusiasm on to his sons, whom he also taught to fish and shoot—field sports that Ernest practised with delight and skill throughout his life.

At school Hemingway was a good all-rounder, taking part in games, debates, music, drama, writing for the school magazine, and making a respectable showing at his academic work. As an older boy he went off on camping expeditions, catching trout, shooting game-birds, and learning to become self-reliant. In short, he was a talented, energetic young man, who gave a good account of himself in a highly competitive world. In 1917 he volunteered for active service in the United States Army, only to be rejected because of slightly defective sight in his left eye. After a brief apprenticeship as a newspaper reporter, learning how to tell a story clearly and swiftly, he volunteered for service with an American Red Cross ambulance unit on the Italian front, and in May 1918 sailed for Europe and some of the most formative, if at the same time catastrophic, experiences of his life.

The first of these occurred when he reached Italy. There was an explosion at an ammunition factory on the outskirts of Milan. Hemingway's unit assisted in taking the injured to hospital, and, more grimly, in removing fragments of human flesh from the remains of the factory's barbed-wire perimeter fence. For an imaginative youngster, not yet nineteen, this experience was profoundly shocking. Worse was to follow a few weeks later when he was severely wounded by a fragmentation shell while distributing Red Cross supplies to Italian troops in the front line. The explosion knocked him out: later he wrote that it was as if a blast-furnace door had swung open and, unable to breathe in the roaring blast, he had rushed bodily out of himself and for a moment knew that he was dead. When he recovered consciousness, in spite of extensive leg injuries he carried a wounded Italian soldier on his back to a first aid post, sustaining further injury from heavy machine-gun bullets as he did so. After emergency treatment he was sent to a hospital where, in the course of twelve operations, the surgeons removed over two hundred fragments of metal from his body and legs.

This direct experience of physical wounding affected not only his life but all that he was to write, serving as one introduction to a 'world of reality overshadowed by violence and death'. The wounds he sustained were not only physical but also emotional in their effect; and soon he sustained further emotional wounds of a different kind. He fell romantically in love with an American nurse, who, some months later, when he was convalescing back home in America, wrote to say that she was by now in love with an Italian officer. Here again Hemingway came up against an area of painful reality, which provided themes he was to seek to explore in his writing.

In 1919 he became a newspaper reporter in Toronto, moving to Paris as European correspondent at the end of 1921, shortly after his first marriage. During these years he was experimenting with poetry and short story writing, and engaged in earnest discussion of literary craftsmanship and techniques with other writers. In Paris he met such notable authors as James Joyce (1882-1941), Ezra Pound (1885-1972), and Gertrude Stein (1874-1946), besides young aspiring writers including F. Scott Fitzgerald (1896-1940). His newspaper work took him to Switzerland, Germany, Italy, Spain, Greece and Turkey, where he covered economic and political conferences, witnessed the brutalities of the Greco-Turkish war, and observed the growth of Fascist and Communist movements. His reports on these subjects were accompanied by occasional lighter articles, accounts of fishing holidays, winter sports, and the social scene in Paris. He was also acquiring material which could be worked up into short stories or serve as incidents or background for his novels. He was, however, aware of the danger of blunting the impact, and of dissipating the emotional significance, of these varied experiences through having to write them up immediately. To put them on paper was in a way to lose them. Since he had high ambitions as a creative literary artist, he decided to give up journalism and concentrate on his own fiction.

In 1923 he published in Paris his first book, *Three Stories and Ten Poems,* which attracted the notice of critics and publishers on the look-out for new talent, as did *In our time* (1924), a collection of brief, highly compressed experimental sketches or vignettes. *In Our Time,* a collection of fifteen short stories interleaved with these vignettes, was published in New York in 1925.

This volume brought his work to the attention of a wider public and introduced his readers for the first time to the 'Hemingway hero'. Seven of the stories have as their central character a young American called Nick Adams. Together they form a series of episodes, rather like loosely connected fragments of a biographical novel, in which Nick Adams suffers various traumatic experiences. These range from witnessing suicide to being wounded by machine-gun fire, and from being disillusioned in adolescent love to contact with a disturbing underworld of punch-drunk boxers, hired killers, homosexuals, and whores. What we are called upon to witness is the hero's loss of innocence and his introduction to the reality of pain and suffering. The world is not a good and comfortable place, as he had been brought up to expect; on the contrary it contains much that is evil and discomforting. The Hemingway hero, in the various guises in which he is presented in these and later stories and novels, is a man who bears both physical and psychological scars: Robert Jordan, in *For Whom The Bell Tolls,* is one of the major examples. Hemingway's chief preoccupation in all his writing is how men are to live with such scars.

The solution is to be found in a moral code of behaviour. Hemingway criticism has referred to this as 'the heroic code' and has described it as the exhibition of 'grace under pressure'. It is useful to get a firm grasp of what is meant by these ideas in order fully to understand Hemingway's work.

The elements of the code may be summarised as follows: avoidance of self-pity; courageous acceptance of disasters which one has not necessarily brought upon oneself; intellectual and emotional honesty in dealing with one's own affairs and with other people; tenderness and compassion for the weak, the vulnerable, and the inexperienced; the cultivation of gaiety of spirit rather than gloom or despair; recourse to ironic humour about one's predicaments rather than recourse to bitterness, recrimination, or tears. In *For Whom The Bell Tolls* we shall find these articles of the heroic code exemplified not only in the central characters of Robert Jordan and Pilar, the experienced, unsentimental, tough-minded but tender-hearted gypsy woman, but also in other minor characters at moments when they are under pressure and behave with courage, honour, and grace.

A year after *In Our Time* was published Hemingway had the manuscripts of two more novels ready. *The Torrents of Spring* (1926), a satirical burlesque of the contemporary literary scene in the United States, caused a stir on that scene at the time but was soon forgotten: it remains a minor book and untypical of Hemingway's work. The other novel, published in America as *The Sun Also Rises* (1926) and in England as *Fiesta* (1927), finally established Hemingway as a major twentieth-century writer.

This novel is set in the café society of the Left Bank (the university quarter) of Paris in the 1920s, a mixture of actual and would-be artists, writers, intellectuals, and social celebrities, together with a crowd of hangers-on. The story is focused on the relationship between Jake Barnes, a hardworking American newspaperman who has been emasculated by a war wound, and the woman with whom he is deeply but helplessly in love, Lady Brett Ashley, an Englishwoman whose fiancé has been killed in the war. Brett has developed into an irresponsible alcoholic and nymphomaniac, and is waiting to marry an Englishman of her own kind after his divorce. The plotting of these frustrated relationships is complicated by further sub-plots involving other characters who are attracted to Brett. After involvement with a playboy novelist and a Spanish bull-fighter she rejects them all, accepting with clear-sighted honesty the hopelessness of the situation in which she finds herself. Though apparently condemned to remain in an emotional and physical waste land, Brett still exhibits some redeeming graces. Jake too achieves ultimate moral strength as he learns to cope with his own disastrous situation, holding on with a kind of desperate acceptance despite his physical and emotional wounds. Readers of this novel will find a number of elements in the portrayal of Jake Barnes which foreshadow elements in the portrayal of Robert Jordan. These include a fatalistic acceptance of one's troubles as just so much bad luck; private rituals and routines to distract the mind from brooding on one's fears; the extension of comfort and reassurance to others who are weaker or less courageous than oneself; and a kind of instinctive understanding which is shared by those who have experienced the same extreme pressures and have withstood them decently and honourably.

Hemingway's next novel, *A Farewell to Arms* (1929), is a romantic tragedy of love and war which he fabricated around two of the shattering experiences he had undergone in Italy, firstly being wounded in the Austrian attack, and secondly the love affair with the hospital nurse which ended so painfully. Transforming these themes into fiction, he wrote a carefully constructed novel which shows considerable advances in his literary technique. The book is divided into five parts, in the first of which we meet Frederic, a young American serving with an Italian ambulance unit, and Catherine, the British nurse with whom he embarks on an affair that is for both of them casual and cold-blooded. This section ends with a description of the hero's being wounded in the legs and sent to hospital in Milan. In the second part the two fall truly and whole-heartedly in love: when Frederic returns to the front they regard themselves as effectively man and wife. Part three is a gripping description of the rout of the Italian army at Caporetto. Frederic finds himself in danger of being shot as a suspected enemy agent disguised in Italian uniform, and saves his skin by deserting. In section four he is reunited with Catherine who is pregnant. Together they flee to Switzerland to avoid Frederic's arrest as a deserter. In the final section Catherine dies in childbirth, leaving Frederic as the scarred survivor of this tale of war time love.

Again there are elements in this novel which readers of *For Whom The Bell Tolls* will recognise. These include the author's intense interest in military matters; his obsession with wounding and death; and such ideas as the necessity to accept that pain, misfortune, and cruelty fall impartially on the good and the gentle as well as on the bad and the violent. Two technical features should also be noticed. One is the use of extended metaphor and simile, as for instance in the comparison of a doomed army to ants swarming to their death on a burning camp fire log. In *For Whom The Bell Tolls* we find this technique used in Chapter 19 when Pilar describes the odour of death which gypsies detect surrounding a doomed man, and again in Chapters 7, 13 and 37 to convey the sensations of the sexual communion and ecstasy shared by Jordan and Maria. The second technical feature is Hemingway's use of recurrent symbols to set the mood of various scenes and episodes. In *A Farewell to Arms* skilful use is made of weather symbolism. The rain that sets a sombre mood in the first chapter falls again during the retreat from Caporetto and pelts down in Switzerland when Catherine is dying, whereas the idyllic love interlude in Milan lasts through the warm summer nights and ends with the first chill of autumn when Frederic returns to the front. This identification of contrasting weather with contrasting moods adds a symbolic forewarning of doom when Catherine casually mentions that she is 'afraid of the rain because sometimes I see me dead in it'. In the same way, in *For Whom The Bell Tolls* Hemingway uses the arrival of enemy aircraft both as a bad sign in a directly literal sense, and also as a symbolic omen of doom, particularly in a passage of deliberately contrived ambiguity in Chapter 13 (see the detailed summaries in Part 2 for further comment).

During the period when he was publishing these novels Hemingway continued to write short stories, many of which appeared in magazines before being collected in book form under the titles *Men Without Women* (1927) and *Winner Take Nothing* (1933), followed by the later collection *The Short Stories of Ernest Hemingway* (1938). This contained in addition the text of his unsuccessful play *The Fifth Column*, set in the Spanish Civil War. He also contributed occasional articles to various journals, mainly on travel and sport: after a painful divorce and remarriage he had taken up big-game hunting in Africa and deep-sea fishing in the Caribbean to add to his earlier interest in bull-fighting.

His next book, *Death in the Afternoon* (1932), said by many to be one of the best introductions to Spanish bull-fighting ever written, is worth reading for other reasons also. Discursive and entertaining, it contains reflections on a multitude of topics, not least on the craft of fiction and on Hemingway's own preoccupations and aims as a writer. This was followed by *Green Hills of Africa* (1935), an account of a hunting safari in Kenya which, though essentially a volume of description and personal reminiscence, is constructed like a novel. It too contains literary criticism and judgments, presented in the course of reported conversations in camp and through the author's reflections on the books he admires and on his own writing.

The effects of the economic depression in the early 1930s, the growth of Fascism in Mussolini's Italy and Hitler's Germany, and the events leading to the Spanish Civil War, brought Hemingway back to an involvement with political and social issues. Another war for democracy was clearly on the way. Hemingway's independent and self-reliant personality made it unthinkable for him to commit himself politically to Marxism, as many European and American writers did at that time. But he went to Spain as a war correspondent, personally raised money for ambulances for the Republican side, and turned to themes of economic injustice in his next novel, *To Have and Have Not* (1937). This was put together from two long magazine stories to which he added a third section, a sub-plot, and other background material. It recounts the adventures and final death of an ex-policeman turned liquor smuggler, who, despite attempts to earn an honest living, is forced once more into crime, this time smuggling illegal immigrants from Cuba to the United States, in order to feed his family when his employer decamps, owing him several hundred dollars. This is not one of Hemingway's best novels; but it does show new developments in his technique. In it he experimented with devices for enlarging the reader's view of the central character, who is presented in Part One in the first person, in Part Two in the third, and in Part Three in a combination of first person narration by a minor character, third person narrative, and stream of consciousness passages flowing through the minds of the central character and his wife. In *For Whom The Bell Tolls,* his next novel, Hemingway carried this technique further, enlarging the span of time and space by admitting the reader to the streams of thought passing through Jordan's mind, and by making Pilar, Maria, and other characters give accounts of their experiences before the action of the novel.

By the time *For Whom The Bell Tolls* (1940) was published, the Second World War had already begun. When eventually the United States of America entered the war Hemingway, then living in Cuba, fitted out his motor launch as an auxiliary patrol boat and cruised the

Caribbean in search of enemy submarines. Later he went to London as a war correspondent, flew as an observer with the Royal Air Force, crossed to France with the invasion forces, and followed the campaign into Germany. These years were not immediately productive of literary work. His energies and emotions were otherwise engaged, not only in war but also in separation from his third wife (whom he had met during the Spanish Civil War) and in contracting his happy fourth marriage. After the war he did, however, set his hand to a long wartime novel. This was published after his death as *The Island and the Stream* (1970). Although it is well planned and contains some superb writing, overall it falls short of his best work, probably because he did not himself give the manuscript his customary final revision, a task to which he always brought great technical skill and the critical intelligence of a supreme artist. His other posthumous publication, *A Moveable Feast* (1964), is better finished. An entertaining and interesting series of sketches of his literary apprenticeship in Paris, it sheds further light on his views on literature and life.

In the immediate postwar years Hemingway's health gave him and his doctors some anxiety. He had suffered two major concussions during the war, and had neglected to rest after them. The second concussion left him for a time with double vision. He continued to have severe headaches and impaired powers of concentration. Then on a visit to Italy in 1948 he had further trouble with infection spreading from a scratch on his left eye. It was feared that the poison might reach his brain, though fortunately this was averted by massive doses of penicillin. The potential dangers, however, were deeply disturbing for an imaginative man who was ambitious about his performance as a writer and literary artist; and there seems little doubt that these anxieties left a permanent mark on his emotional health. Worse still was to come in 1954 when he was on safari in East Africa. In two light aircraft accidents in two days he was fully concussed again, sustained head, spinal and internal injuries, and suffered extensive first degree burns. That disaster however lay in the future.

In 1950 Hemingway published *Across The River and Into The Trees*. This again is an uneven novel. It contains some of his most intense descriptive writing, especially in the opening chapter which describes a day's duck shooting in the Venetian marshes; but there are passages in which he presents the hero, a war-battered US Army colonel, through descriptions of minor behaviour and through dialogue which strike many readers as bordering on the ludicrous, perhaps because they do not fully achieve their purpose as symbolic illuminations of character. The novel, however, contains a development of Hemingway's heroic code. This tale of the love affair between an ageing colonel facing death from a heart attack and a young Venetian countess facing life with her heart attacked in a metaphorical sense, recapitulates the code's message of personal redemption through courage, tenderness, and grace under pressure. But there is also an additional hint at the parallel message of Christian grace and redemption, to show that the code is a rule of life that bestows the power to face and even to conquer the final fact of death. This philosophical parallelism was carried further in the last work Hemingway published before his own death. So also were the new technical experiments he tried out in *Across The River and Into The Trees,* to which he gave a closely knit sub-structure of symbolism. Readers who turn to it should look for such symbolic parallels as those between the Colonel's inadequate heart muscle and an underpowered motor-boat engine; between the varying levels of the tides under the Venetian canal bridges, the levels of the colonel's blood pressure and cardiac condition, and the levels of the lovers' emotions; and so forth.

If Hemingway did not handle these multiple functions of symbolism entirely successfully in this novel, he achieved perfection in *The Old Man and The Sea* (1952). This is the most closely-organised book he ever wrote, in which the story of an old fisherman's single-handed fight with a giant marlin, at one level a direct, intense action narrative, is at the same time an allegory of life and death, hope and salvation, art and its pursuit, whose symbolism operates continuously at multiple levels of meaning. The final message, that a man can be destroyed but not defeated, was to be borne out by Hemingway's own fate.

On 21 July 1961 Ernest Hemingway committed suicide at his last home in Ketchum, Idaho, by blowing out his brains with a double-barrelled shotgun. His health had been deteriorating for some time and he was no longer able to write. He had just been brought back from hospital after a prolonged but ineffective series of treatments for high blood pressure and acute nervous depression. The writer had been destroyed, and so the man destroyed what was left of himself. But he had not been defeated: the victories he had won as an artist still remain in his work.

A note on the text

For Whom The Bell Tolls was first published by Charles Scribner's Sons, New York, 1940, and Jonathan Cape, London, 1941. Page references in Parts 3 and 4 of these Notes are to the two most readily available British paperback editions. P = Penguin Books, Harmondsworth 1955; TP = Triad/Panther Books, Frogmore, St Albans, 1976.

A film version, starring Gary Cooper as Jordan and Ingrid Bergman as Maria, was released by Paramount Pictures in 1943.

Part 2

Summaries

of FOR WHOM THE BELL TOLLS

A general summary

The action of the novel is centred on a sabotage operation behind the Fascist lines during the Spanish Civil War. Robert Jordan, an American university professor of Spanish who is fighting on the side of the Republican government, has been charged with the mission of blowing up a bridge so as to prevent the movement of Fascist troops against a Republican offensive. The timing of the bridge demolition is crucial to the success of the offensive, which has been planned by a Russian general called Golz. Jordan knows that his chances of getting away after the operation are slight.

Jordan and an elderly peasant called Anselmo base themselves on a guerilla band in the mountains. The morale of the guerillas is low. Pablo, their leader, is more devoted to saving his own skin than to saving the Republic; but Pablo's woman, Pilar, who has great influence on the rest of the band, supports Jordan. The band includes a young girl, Maria, who has been raped and tortured by Fascist soldiers: she is under Pilar's special protection. Jordan and Maria become lovers, with Pilar's approval. The safety of the guerillas is threatened, firstly by a snowstorm, and secondly when a Fascist cavalryman rides into the camp and has to be shot: enemy patrols will naturally be sent out to look for him.

Another guerilla leader, El Sordo, has promised to support Jordan. A cavalry patrol tracks him down and El Sordo and his men fight it out until they are killed by Fascist bomber planes. Anselmo is sent to the nearest town and returns with news that Golz's plan of attack has been leaked and is common gossip. Jordan sends a messenger through the lines to ask Golz to call off the attack. Meantime he must continue with his plans.

Pablo disappears that night, taking Jordan's detonators for the explosives with him. Next morning he returns, confesses to having thrown the detonators away in a moment of cowardice, and helps Jordan to improvise new detonators from hand-grenades. Jordan's messenger arrives at Golz's headquarters too late to have the attack called off. When they hear the Republican bombers attacking the enemy lines, Jordan and Pablo's band destroy the bridge and its guard posts. As they cross the road on their escape route through the mountains, Jordan is mortally wounded. Maria wishes to stay with him, but he sends her on under Pilar's care. The novel closes as Jordan covers the guerillas' escape with his machine gun in the last minutes of his life.

This summary is designed to give the reader an outline of the main action of the story and to introduce the major characters. The novel is, however, complex in its construction and its range of reference, and contains many minor characters both within the guerilla bands and in other events recalled and recounted by the major characters. This wide range of reference is explained in detail, together with the many Spanish and other language phrases and references, in the chapter summaries that follow. Before turning to them, the reader should be sure of having a clear view of the political background of the novel. This is as follows.

After a series of changing governments in a confused political situation between 1918 and 1923, the King of Spain was forced to suspend the constitution and to accept a military directorate under the presidency of Primo de Rivera, who later, as Premier, lost the support of the Army. In 1931 municipal elections followed by a general election swept the Republican party into power, and the King left the country. The centre-right Republican Government was, however, perpetually under attack from both the Monarchists on the right and the Communists and Anarchists on the left. In the February 1936 election the left-wing Popular Front gained power. There was rioting in the streets between the extreme right, mainly the Falangist party, and the extreme left. In July civil war broke out between the right, under the leadership of General Franco, and the elected government, whose supporters are referred to as Republicans or Loyalists. Both sides gained support from outside Spain, the Falangists from volunteer units from the Fascist dictatorships of Germany and Italy, the Republicans from Stalin's USSR and the left-wing volunteers from many countries who formed the Communist-led International Brigades. The action of *For Whom The Bell Tolls* takes place against this political background. Jordan and the guerillas are fighting for the Republicans, and their operation is part of an attack planned against Franco's troops.

It is suggested that students should read each chapter summary before reading the chapter itself. The chapter should then be read using the notes to explain difficulties in the text. For some students a re-reading of the summary will help to fix the development of the novel before going on to the next chapter.

Detailed summaries

Chapter 1

A young man, Robert Jordan, lies hidden in a pine forest in the mountains. He looks down at a road, a river, and a mill, trying to see the bridge marked on his copy of a military map. An old peasant called Anselmo is with him. They discuss the bridge and the sentry posts guarding it, one in the sawmill, which is above the bridge, the other in a roadmender's hut below the bridge. There are also two sentries on the bridge itself. Then they climb to a camp above. Jordan is a Republican partizan working as a dynamiter behind the Fascist lines. As they climb he recalls the Russian General Golz explaining an attack to be made by his troops, and how Jordan must blow up the bridge at a precise moment in the operation so as to stop enemy reinforcements. Golz and Jordan are both anxious about the chances of success.

When Jordan and Anselmo reach the camp Anselmo brings Pablo, the leader of the guerilla band, to meet Jordan. Pablo cannot read Jordan's identity papers. Suspicious and unfriendly, he wants to take Jordan's dynamite for his own use. He knows that if the bridge is blown up his band will be hunted out of the mountains. Anselmo is angry with Pablo and tells him to carry Jordan's packs. Pablo's sad and sullen manner worries Jordan. He pleases Pablo by praising the horses Pablo has captured; but when Pablo asks for news of another dynamiter, Kashkin, and learns that he is dead, Pablo says they will all end up like that. Jordan reflects on Pablo's possible treachery, contrasting it with Anselmo's reliability and loyalty, as they approach the camp.

NOTES AND GLOSSARY:

Barco de Avila: a town in the province of Avila, about one hundred and fifty kilometres west of Madrid

La Granja: a town in the Sierra de Guadarrama mountains. Golz's attack is designed to capture this important road junction on the way to Segovia

the Escorial: a sixteenth century royal palace outside Madrid, containing a magnificent library, monastery and cathedral

Comrade General Golz: a Russian general in command of the attack through the Sierra de Guadarrama. Golz jokes with Jordan about the Spanish pronunciation of J and G as aspirates, turning Jordan's name into a pun on 'whore down'

Vicente Rojo:	a Spanish Republican general, Chief of Staff in Madrid
Segovia:	capital of the province of Segovia, some seventy kilometres north-west of Madrid; the objective of the offensive in the spring of 1937 of which Golz's attack was a part
Guadarrama:	a town under the Sierra of that name
Navacerrada:	a village in the Sierra
Salud, Camarada:	*(Spanish)* Greetings, comrade
Quevedo:	Francisco Gómez Quevedo y Villegas (1590-1645), seventeenth-century Spanish political satirist and poet
picket pins:	stakes for tethering horses
alpargatas:	*(Spanish)* rope-soled sandals
Velasquez:	Diego de Silva y Velasquez (1599-1660), seventeenth-century Spanish Court painter
cannon-bone:	bone between the hough (knee) and fetlock (ankle) of a horse
vaquero:	*(Spanish)* mounted cattle-herdsman, whence the American cowboy *buckaroo*
guardia civil:	*(Spanish)* police
Arevalo:	town on the main railway line from Madrid to Segovia
Sierra de Gredos:	mountain range in Avila, west of Madrid
Moors:	troops from Spanish Morocco, at whose head General Franco rebelled against the Republican Government
Jockey Club:	an exclusive racehorse-owners' club, responsible for the management of flat-racing
Il a manqué son Jockey:	*(French)* he has failed to make his Jockey, to be elected to the Jockey Club. But the phrase is ambiguous, and Jordan is also referring to the well-known joke about the homosexual racehorse owner whose advances to a jockey were rejected

---

Chapter 2

Jordan sees that the camp, with a cave for living quarters, is well hidden from aircraft but badly guarded. A gypsy, Rafael, is carving sticks to make a trap. He boasts that he will destroy a tank, but Anselmo says gypsies talk big and do little: Rafael admits that even in war gypsies keep on being gypsies. Pablo joins them and asks further about Kashkin's death: when he was with the guerillas he had asked to be shot if wounded rather than be allowed to fall into Fascist hands.

Jordan knows the manner of Kashkin's death but keeps it to himself. A girl carries food from the cave. She is tall and beautiful but her hair has been cropped short. Jordan, attracted to her, learns that her hair was shaved when she was a prisoner of the Fascists: Pablo's band rescued her when they blew up a train. Her name is Maria and she is no one's woman. Jordan is told of Pablo's woman, Pilar, brave but ugly and much respected by the guerillas. It was she who insisted that they bring back Maria from the train. Rafael discloses that Pilar has gypsy blood and second sight. She appears, and she and Jordan take to each other at once, recognising bravery and loyalty in each other. Pilar says Pablo has lost his courage. She also warns Jordan to treat Maria gently. She reads his hand to tell his future, but unsmilingly refuses to say what she reads there. She suggests they seek the aid of El Sordo, another guerilla leader, after Jordan and Anselmo have inspected the bridge.

NOTES AND GLOSSARY:

Hola: (Spanish) Hello

resinous from the wineskin: tasting of the pine resin used to seal the wineskin

Valladolid: one of the first cities to fall to the Fascist rebels

Estremadura: region in south-west Spain towards Portugal

mujer: (Spanish) woman, wife

muy floyo: (Spanish) very slack, or as Anselmo repeats, very flaccid. Hemingway uses the device of repeating Spanish phrases in translation throughout the dialogue: in this chapter see, for instance, *Me voy, no es nada* and *borracho.*

matador de toros: bull-fighter

Lewis gun: machine-gun notorious for its mechanism being jammed by the cartridges

máquina: (Spanish) machine, here the gun

Inglés: (Spanish) English

El Sordo: (Spanish) literally, the deaf man

. . . a name I can never dominate: one of the many examples of Hemingway's use of Latin- or Spanish-derived words and idioms to give the impression of foreign speech. The standard English phrase would be 'a name I can never master'

the Republic: the Republican government or loyalist side, as opposed to the rebel nationalist or Fascist side

But now he is terminated: another example of Spanish-flavoured idiom: standard English, 'finished'

Valencia: important city on the east coast

Chapter 3

Jordan makes a drawing of the bridge to work out how to blow it up. He examines one of the sentries, a man with a peasant's face, through his field glasses. Jordan and Anselmo (also a peasant) discuss the sentries and their movements. As they return they see aircraft overhead; they are probably enemy planes, Jordan thinks privately. Anselmo talks happily of the days after the war, when he will again hunt animals, not men. Killing men is a sin. The free-thinking Republic has abolished the Church and Anselmo misses the comforts of religion; but he hates the cruelty of the nationalists who claim to be the defenders of Christianity. Rather than kill his enemies, Anselmo would wish to educate them by making them work like ordinary people; but in war he must sometimes kill and he will carry out Jordan's orders. Jordan reflects bitterly on Golz's attack and the dangers for good men like Anselmo. Deliberately he turns his thoughts to Maria. Agustín, one of the sentries guarding Pablo's camp, challenges them. He has forgotten the password, and is ill-disciplined and foul-mouthed. He asks if it is true that they are to blow up the bridge, and warns Jordan to guard his dynamite carefully. Anselmo tells Jordan that Agustín is reliable, unlike Pablo: he too says they must guard the dynamite.

NOTES AND GLOSSARY:

monoplanes: aircraft with one set of wings. In the 1930s many aircraft were biplanes, which had two sets of wings

Moscas: *(Spanish)* literally, flies

a formidable aviation: a strong Air Force. Another example of an idiom derived from the Spanish

the boar, the bear, the wolf, the ibex: these, and the eagle mentioned below, are all animals whose fighting skill and courage are a fair match for the hunter's skill and courage

Let *them* have God: 'they' are the Fascists

Mausers: repeating rifles

Uncock thy piece: reset the bolt of the rifle so that the trigger can not fire it: Spanish-derived idiom

obscene bridge . . . obscenely well obscenity ourselves off: Hemingway's representation of the language of one who habitually swears. Compare 'Go to the unprintable . . . and unprint thyself'; and similar usages throughout the novel. There is a certain ironic humour in this technique

Chapter 4

In the dark outside the cave Jordan unlocks his packs and checks that his equipment is all safe. On second thoughts he brings the packs into the cave. Pablo objects but Jordan insists. There are other members of Pablo's band there. Jordan recognises tension and hostility in their behaviour, even from Rafael the gypsy. Pablo accepts Jordan's cigarettes but commits a breach of hospitality by saying he cannot spare any wine for Jordan. Jordan calls Maria to bring him a cup of water into which he pours absinthe from his flask, refusing to give Pablo any. (The absinthe nostalgically reminds him of pre-war visits to Paris.) Pablo says his people will not blow up the bridge. Jordan ignores him and is supported by Anselmo. He appeals to Pilar. She supports Jordan's plan: the rest of the band support her against Pablo, who predicts disaster. In the mounting tension Jordan unobtrusively gets his pistol ready to shoot Pablo if necessary. Pilar sends Maria outside to spare her a possible scene of violence, but Pablo submits and Jordan explains the details of his plan. Pilar herself feels no sense of triumph, only a sense of doom. They eat their supper.

NOTES AND GLOSSARY:

grummet:	a rope ring
exploder:	the firing device
caps:	the detonators for the explosion of the dynamite
anis, absinthe:	aniseed-flavoured liqueur
Parc Montsouris . . .:	images of the Paris Hemingway later recreated in *A Moveable Feast*
Serrano ham:	a dry-cured Spanish ham, eaten raw like Parma or Bayonne ham
a seed bull:	bulls raised for breeding (and by implication not for brains)
Buenas, Compadre:	*(Spanish)* Well, my friend
Chico:	*(Spanish)* a term of affection
la gente:	*(Spanish)* the people; the present company

Chapter 5

Jordan goes out to breathe the night air: it is cold and he thinks it will be frosty later. He hears Rafael singing and playing the guitar until Pablo and Pilar tell him to be quiet. Rafael joins Jordan and asks why he did not kill Pablo during the quarrel: everyone was prepared for it, since Pablo is now a danger to them. Pablo joins them. He tells Jordan to pay no attention to Pilar or to their recent difference of opinion, and says he is glad Jordan has come to join them. Pablo goes off to see to his horses. Jordan follows secretly, brooding over the quarrel in the cave. His first duty is to blow up the bridge: would it have been better to kill Pablo? or for one of Pablo's band to kill him? He sees Pablo talking to one of the horses, but cannot hear what he says. In fact, Pablo is praising the horse, who, he says, does not insult or reject him like Pilar or young Maria.

NOTES AND GLOSSARY:

saffron:	dried crocus flower used in Spanish cooking
pimentos:	large sweet peppers
copper-penny:	a favourite image of Hemingway's when describing how stale air and sweat smell and taste metallic in the mouth
the Catalan:	the song about a man from the province of Catalonia. The special ethnic culture of the Catalans was recognised by the Republic, which gave them self-government in 1932
Qué va:	*(Spanish)* So what!
pueblo:	*(Spanish)* village

Chapter 6

In the cave Jordan talks to Pilar and Maria. Pilar is surprised that El Sordo has not made his usual visit: they will look for him next day. Pilar teases Jordan by asking if he thinks Maria beautiful. They discuss politics. Maria's father was shot for being a life-long Republican. Jordan says his father and grandfather were Republicans (in the United States); he discloses that his father shot himself. Maria feels this to be a bond between them: their mutual attraction develops. Jordan privately asks Maria if he should have killed Pablo, but Pilar says it was not necessary: Pablo is past the point of being dangerous.

NOTES AND GLOSSARY:

Don Roberto . . .:	the comrades in the guerilla band, where all are equal, use these aristocratic titles as a joke
pus:	yellow discharge from a poisoned wound
permanganate:	purple chemical used as an antiseptic. The purple of the Republican flag will cleanse the corrupt colours of the old regime

Chapter 7

Robert Jordan is in his sleeping-bag outside the cave. Maria comes out, wakes him, and climbs in with him. They talk of each other.

Maria fears that Jordan will not love her when she tells him that she was raped by the Fascists. She hopes—as Pilar had suggested—that Jordan's love will erase the memory of this brutal experience. They make love happily. Maria wishes to be Jordan's woman for ever. He says his present work makes such a future impossible; but she is his woman now.

NOTES AND GLOSSARY:

robe: sleeping-bag

little rabbit: pet name or term of endearment

where there had been roughness . . . all was smooth . . .: a lyrical passage, of a kind to be repeated in the novel, in which Hemingway conveys the feelings of love and sexuality more as a poet than a novelist

lo sabes?: *(Spanish)* do you know?

that I was not sick: with venereal disease after being raped by the Fascist soldiers

---

Chapter 8

Jordan wakes to find that Maria has gone to light the fire in the cave. Pablo comes out of the forest where he has been seeing to the horses. A large number of Fascist fighter and bomber planes flies overhead: it is a bad omen. Jordan sends Anselmo to watch the road and report on the movement of military vehicles and troops. Jordan questions Fernando, a member of the band who goes regularly behind the enemy lines to gather information. Fernando says that in La Granja there is much talk of an offensive being prepared by the Republicans: this is to include the blowing up of bridges. Maria and Pilar make jokes at the expense of Fernando, who is a rather simple and literal-minded man. This leads to reminiscences by Pilar about her past life and her stay in Valencia with her former lover, the bull-fighter Finito.

NOTES AND GLOSSARY:

poncho: *(Spanish)* a woollen cloak

Qué más da: *(Spanish)* So what

Fiats: Italian fighter aircraft

Heinkel one-elevens: type of German medium bomber

in echelons: moving in parallel lines but stepped so as to give each unit a clear field of fire

in echelon of echelons: a complex arrangement of echelons, as further explained in the text by Hemingway

chasers: pursuit planes, fighters

Junkers: type of German heavy bomber

Colmenar:	village fifteen kilometres north of Madrid
Manzanares el Real:	near the Escorial
dummy planes:	full-scale models of aircraft
props:	propellers
sweating the big drop:	sweating with fear of the bombing
camions:	*(French)* lorries, trucks
power plant:	for electricity
hombre:	*(Spanish)* man. A common form of address in Spanish conversation
Quiepo de Llano:	Spanish General on the nationalist side who frequently spoke on the radio to the Spanish people
Alto del Leon:	*(Spanish)* literally, the Height of the Lion
Como siempre:	*(Spanish)* As usual
Vamos!:	*(Spanish)* Come on, then! Well, now!
Feria:	*(Spanish)* the annual fair, held in Valencia at the end of July
paella:	*(Spanish)* a Spanish dish of rice with vegetables, meat or fish
traca:	*(Spanish)* continuous line or chain (here, of fireworks)

Chapter 9

More planes fly over, the last of them low enough to see the horses and perhaps the cave. Pilar and Jordan talk of Maria. Pilar wants Jordan to take Maria away with him. She speaks of Pablo, who in the night had wept with shame and confessed his fear of death. Jordan tells Pilar that he is deeply in love with Maria. Pilar approves and says she will leave Maria with him that evening since they must make the most of their time together. She denies that there is any truth in reading fortunes in the palm of the hand. Jordan shows his affection for Pilar. Pilar, in a formal exchange of swearing and obscenity with Agustín, puts him in charge of Jordan's packs. Agustín tells Pilar that Pablo, though now a coward, is the only man in the band smart enough to lead them to safety after the bridge is blown up.

NOTES AND GLOSSARY:

Gulf Stream:	the warm current flowing from the Gulf of Mexico
guapa:	*(Spanish)* beauty, sweetheart
You may take two where you go:	lead both Maria and Pilar to their death when blowing up the bridge
Don Juan Tenorio:	the legendary seducer of women
novio:	*(Spanish)* betrothed, fiancé

sin picardia: (*Spanish*) literally, without deceit, truly, no joking

the eddy of his own weakness: Agustín compares Pablo to an object floating passively in a river, but predicts that in the coming crisis he will swim swiftly away

---

Chapter 10

Pilar, Maria and Jordan rest as they go to El Sordo's. Pilar seeks to educate her young friends from her own experience of human emotions and relations. Jordan leads her to talk of how she came to know Pablo. She recounts the tale of Pablo's attack on a provincial town at the beginning of the Civil War. It is a tale of courage and skill, but also violence and brutality. The police were deliberately terrorised before being shot by a firing squad. Prominent Fascists in the town were led out from their club one by one and forced to walk between two lines of peasants armed with flails, pitchforks and sickles. The peasants beat them and flung them to their death over a cliff into the river. The victors then turned to looting, drunkenness and violence: they stormed the club and murdered the rest of the prisoners, including the priest who heard their last confessions. Pilar's account shows that courage, terror, dignity, brutality are exhibited in varying degrees and combinations by individuals on both sides of the conflict: 'the people of this town are as kind as they can be cruel'. That night Pablo the victor, and Pilar his woman, felt dehumanised by the brutality they had seen and shared in. Pablo is literally dehumanised, unmanned, and can not make love; Pilar cannot sleep. Pilar hints that the scenes of brutality were repeated three days later when the Fascists recaptured the town.

NOTES AND GLOSSARY:

Pero, venga: (*Spanish*) Come, now

plaza: (*Spanish*) market place

aperitifs: appetising drinks

the necessary sacraments: religious rituals including confession and absolution of sins

Agua: (*Spanish*) water

out of the box: like a bull released into the bull-ring to be killed

Cabron: (*Spanish*) literally, he-goat; cuckold

balky horse: a horse that shies

canalla: (*Spanish*) rabble, mob

Arriba España!:   (*Spanish*) Up with Spain!

Andalucian: from Andalucia, the southern region of Spain

buen provecho: (*Spanish*) literally, good meal; a phrase said by way of courtesy to one who is about to eat

El Debate: *(Spanish)* a newspaper published by the Society of
                      Jesus, whose property was impounded by the
                      Republic in 1932
vermouth and seltzer: wine-based aperitif with soda water
have a belly-full: have more than enough
Viva la Anarquia! . . . Viva la Libertad! (Spanish) Long live
                      Anarchy! . . . Long live Liberty!
Corrida: *(Spanish)* bull-fight
Fonda: *(Spanish)* inn

Chapter 11

On reaching El Sordo's camp they are challenged by a young sentry,
Joaquín, one of those who had rescued Maria from the train. Before
the war he was a shoe-shine boy with ambitions to be a bull-fighter.
His parents were shot by the Fascists in Valladolid. Jordan reflects
that he has heard such events stated baldly many times; but Pilar, a
gifted story-teller, made everything seem so real when she described
the attack on Pablo's town that he felt as if he had been there himself.
If he survives the war he will write a book, trying to describe what he
has known and seen as skilfully as Pilar. He continues to reflect on the
character of the Spanish people and his own reasons for taking part in
the war. He thinks of Maria and his love affair which seems almost as
unreal as a dream. Yet Maria is truly real. Joaquín recounts the fate of
his family and is comforted by Maria and the others.

Jordan and Pilar meet El Sordo (his real name is Santiago) and
discuss the bridge. El Sordo is worried by the planes and troop
movements. He would like to blow up the bridge and escape at once.
There are not enough horses nor enough reliable men, but he has
ammunition and dynamite. He asks how Pablo is: he knows Pablo has
lost his courage. They discuss where they should make for after
dynamiting the bridge. Kashkin's name is mentioned and Jordan tells
El Sordo that he is dead. He was badly wounded when they blew up a
train together and could not move. Jordan shot him at his own request
to save him from the Fascists. The final scene shows the reactions of
Pilar and El Sordo when they consider the slender chance of escaping
after blowing up the bridge: after some tension between them, Jordan
and El Sordo are allies.

NOTES AND GLOSSARY:
'You're growing the pigtail now': the pigtail worn by bull-fighters
Eleventh Brigade: one of the International Brigades of volunteers on
                      the government side. Hans was one of their
                      generals

Garbo . . . Harlow . . . Jack Gilbert: Greta Garbo and Jean Harlow
were famous film actresses of the 1930s. John
Gilbert was leading man in several Garbo films

Pozoblanco: town in Cordoba, scene of an early incident in the
events leading up to the Civil War

corrales: *(Spanish)* fenced enclosures, farm yards

cortijos: *(Spanish)* farm-houses

Deja: *(Spanish)* Drop it; cut it out

horseholders: men to hold the horses while Jordan and the
guerillas blow up the bridge

algo raro, pero bueno: (Spanish) a bit strange, but good

Como fué?: *(Spanish)* How was it?

goat crut: the dung of goats

Chapter 12

Pilar, Maria and Jordan walk home. Pilar is tired and has to rest. She
caresses Maria and demonstrates her love for the girl, promising that
Jordan shall have her later. She confesses to being jealous of Maria's
youth. An experienced woman, she speaks frankly and bluntly, saying
that if she herself were young she could take Jordan from Maria. But
her mood returns to realism: there is little time, and she leaves the
young lovers alone.

NOTES AND GLOSSARY:

tortillera: *(Spanish)* pervert, lesbian

por qué: *(Spanish)* Why

Chapter 13

Jordan and Maria make love: their sensations of ecstasy are presented
in a lyrical paragraph of prose-poetry. Afterwards they speak of their
feelings—happiness is swift, says Maria, as a galloping horse. Or,
Jordan absently says, they 'could take [her] happiness in a plane'.
Maria interprets this in terms of soaring emotion; but the reader has
already seen that planes are a menace to Jordan's task, and the remark
is ambiguous and doom-laden. Jordan is preoccupied with the bridge.
He goes over the operation in his mind. He reflects on his role in
fighting for democracy; on the corruption of some of the Republican
leaders as contrasted with the unselfish virtues of so many Republicans; on his own scorn of political propaganda. He remains independent. He does not wish to die a hero's death: he would prefer to live
out his life with Maria and to take her back to America as his wife
when he returns to his job as a university teacher.

Returning to the present, he thinks of the short time he can realistically count on with Maria, who talks of Pilar's instructions on how to look after a husband. Pilar has told Maria to kill herself rather than fall again into the hands of the Fascists; Maria would prefer that Jordan and she should die together. They catch up with Pilar, who asks Maria how things have been with her. Maria does not want to speak of her experience, but Pilar insists. Jordan eventually understands that Pilar is not being merely inquisitive or vicious. She wishes them to recognise their happiness and good fortune as clearly as possible during the time they have together. As they go towards the camp Pilar says that there will be snow, even though it is already the month of May.

NOTES AND GLOSSARY:

that swine Gomez: probably Zaisser, the German Communist commander of the 13th International Brigade

under Communist discipline: a reference to the Russian intervention on the Republican side against Franco and his German and Italian allies

Lerroux . . . Prieto: Republican Prime Minister and Cabinet Minister respectively

a hard-shelled Baptist: in American terms, a symbol of narrow, bigoted religion

cliché: catch phrase, slogan

Bohemianism: unconventional and individualistic way of life

Mayakovsky: Vladimir Mayakovsky (1894-1930), a Russian revolutionary poet

Thermopylae: site of the battle in which a small band of Spartan soldiers defended the independent city-states of Greece against a vast Persian army in 480 BC

Horatius: Roman who defended the bridge over the River Tiber against Rome's enemy Lars Porsena in 505 BC

the Dutch boy: a reference to the legend of the boy who saved the fields from being flooded by plugging a hole in the sea-wall with his finger

Doctor and Mrs Livingstone I presume: an ironic reference to Henry Morton Stanley's (1841-1904) greeting on finding Dr David Livingstone (1813-73), the Scottish missionary and explorer, who had disappeared in Central Africa

Sun Valley, Idaho Hemingway wrote part of this novel in Sun Valley. The other two places were also known to him

Lope de Vega: Lope Félex de Vega Carpio (1562-1635) a Spanish dramatist

Galdós:	Benito Pérez Galdós (1843-1920), famous Spanish novelist
ticketed as a Red:	labelled as a Communist
the fall term:	the opening of the academic year in the autumn. Here we learn that Jordan is an American university teacher on sabbatical leave
dragging ashes:	a physical experience with no emotional involvement

Now, *ahora, maintenant, heute:* in this passage Jordan, a language teacher, busies himself with synonyms—(English, Spanish, French and German respectively)—perhaps to try to keep his mind from dwelling on his desperate situation

You were gone:	You fell in love

to love, honour and cherish . . .: an echo of the Anglican marriage service

'It was a thing I cannot tell thee': so wonderful it cannot be described

Cali:	Spanish gypsy; itself a gypsy word
Gitanos:	*(Spanish)* gypsies
Busnes:	gypsy word for girls

Chapter 14

It is snowing heavily when they reach the camp. Pablo is pleased because the offensive will be put off. Pablo gets drunk and makes sly remarks about the snow interfering with Jordan's sleeping arrangements. Jordan masters his anger and asks Pablo about his past life. Pablo mentions the bull-fighter, Finito de Palencia; and Pilar, whose memories of Finito in the bull-ring are described, starts to speak of her life with him. In particular she recalls his fear of being wounded, and the scene at a banquet given in his honour by his admirers, when Finito eventually broke down in terror from seeing a bull's head on the wall in front of him. Pilar describes how she tended Finito's scarred and bruised body during the years she lived with him before she took up with Pablo. Rafael the gypsy enters. He has given up watching the enemy posts and Fernando goes to relieve Anselmo.

NOTES AND GLOSSARY:

A mi qué?:	*(Spanish)* What's that to me?
prima-donnaing:	behaving temperamentally, as operatic singers are reputed to do
aviones:	*(Spanish)* aeroplanes
Pyrenees:	mountains in north-east of Spain on the French frontier

Cantabrico:	mountainous region in the extreme north of Spain
moose:	North American elk
arroyero:	presumably a wagoner, perhaps connected with *arrollar,* to roll
Asturia:	mining region in north-west Spain
Zaragoza:	capital of Aragon, east of Madrid
withers:	the ridge of muscle between the shoulders
banderillas:	*(Spanish)* small darts mounted on rods, fixed in pairs into the bull's withers during the bull-fight
arrobas:	*(Spanish)* the arroba is a grain measure weighing just over eleven kilograms
the passion of our former Lord:	Easter week. Religion has been abolished, hence Pilar's use of 'former'
aficionados:	*(Spanish)* bull-fight enthusiasts
manzanilla:	*(Spanish)* dry sherry wine
flamenco:	*(Spanish)* type of Andalusian gypsy song with ecstatic climaxes
Qué sencillo!:	*(Spanish)* How simple!
picador horses:	horses ridden by picadors, men who bait the bulls with lances before the matadors fight them on foot

Chapter 15

Anselmo is faithfully recording the movements of cars on the road; but as he is not sufficiently educated to distinguish between the small cars of local army units and the large cars of the General Staff, nor to see the significance of the latter, his report to Jordan will unfortunately be misleading. He thinks how strange it is that he should have to kill Fascist soldiers, simple Spaniards like himself. He recalls Pablo's former leadership and present decline, and wishes the war was over and himself back home. The scene changes to the interior of the sawmill, where the Fascist soldiers are also talking longingly of home. Anselmo continues to think about the sin of killing, a perpetual problem for him. Jordan joins him. Jordan's spirits rise on talking to the good and trustworthy old man as they return to the camp together.

NOTES AND GLOSSARY:

It had on chains:	on the tyres so as to grip the snow
Fords, Fiats, Opels, Renaults, Citroens:	cars of moderate price
Rolls-Royces, Lancias, Mercedes, Isottas:	expensive cars
Gallegos:	from Galicia in northwest Spain
Lister:	one of the commanders in the International Brigades

Franco:	General Francisco Franco (1892-1975), Nationalist leader who became the Head of State and virtual dictator till his death
altered:	castrated
analfabetos:	*(Spanish)* illiterates
Hola, viejo:	*(Spanish)* Hullo, old one
cigar store Indian:	life-size wooden figures of American Indians were used as signs for tobacconists' shops in the USA and occasionally in Britain. Fernando looked like such a figure as he stood still in the forest
Agincourt:	the Battle of Agincourt, 1415; Henry V of England's defeat of the French
Coolidge:	Calvin Coolidge (1872-1933) President (1923-8) of the United States. Used ironically of someone who lacks enthusiasm

Chapter 16

Pilar tells Jordan that El Sordo has been to the cave and has gone to look for horses. Everyone is in the cave: because it is snowing they have posted no sentries. They talk together, mainly asking Jordan about conditions in the USA. Pablo gets steadily drunk and quarrelsome. He becomes so insulting that finally Agustín hits him; but Pablo is cunning enough not to hit back and thus give Agustín or Jordan an excuse to kill him. He is perhaps not as drunk as he pretends. At the climax of this tense scene Pilar tells Pablo to get out. He goes, saying he will return later.

NOTES AND GLOSSARY:

The Lord and Master:	Pilar sarcastically suggests that Jordan is ordering Maria about as if he were the head of the household
our ex-Lord himself:	Christ, abolished by the Republicans. (See note on 'our former Lord', Chapter 14.) Pilar has caught Jordan's joking reference in his question to Maria: in the New Testament story Mary anointed Christ's feet and wiped them with her hair
pinch-bottle:	triangular whisky bottle with its sides pinched in
Bacchus:	the Greek god of wine
the worm that haunts us:	fear
Estados Unidos:	*(Spanish)* United States
Escoceses:	*(Spanish)* Scotsmen
Los cojones:	*(Spanish)* the testicles
homesteading;	a system of granting land to settlers in the western United States

'And then you would walk on the water': a sarcastic reference to Christ's miracle before his disciples. Pilar has no patience with Pablo's attempts to forget his guilt by drinking

Estoy muy borracho: *(Spanish)* I am very drunk
Sinverguenza: *(Spanish)* shamelessness
Cobarde: *(Spanish)* coward
bicho raro: *(Spanish)* strange insect
salud y cojones: *(Spanish)* Good health and balls
negro . . . blanco: *(Spanish)* black . . . white
Qué te importa: *(Spanish)* What does it matter to you
maricón: *(Spanish)* homosexual

Chapter 17

Even Pilar now thinks that Jordan should kill Pablo, who is capable of killing them to save his skin. Every member of the band votes for it, though Maria objects. Jordan agrees to kill him that night. Just then Pablo enters. Agustín in anger is ready to shoot Pablo but Jordan takes Agustín out and reminds him that he might accidentally detonate the dynamite. Pablo says the snow is stopping and next day it will be clear. He has changed his mind and now approves of their plan for the bridge. Afterwards he will lead them to safety in the Sierra de Gredos. Pilar suspects that Pablo has been listening at the door to their decision to kill him.

NOTES AND GLOSSARY:

Matarlo: *(Spanish)* kill him
can make a bureaucracy with his mouth: a reference to Fernando's committee-style of speech, which she parodies a moment later when handing him the bowl of stew
Estoy listo: *(Spanish)* I am ready
monkey business: fooling about
Por favor: *(Spanish)* please
aneroid: type of barometer, for measuring air pressure
manicomio: *(Spanish)* lunatic asylum

Chapter 18 ˙

Jordan reflects uneasily on these rapid turns of events. He makes sketches showing exactly how to blow up the bridge and writes out the plan of attack on the sentry posts. Maria watches him admiringly but uncomprehendingly. When he has finished, Pablo says that he too has been making plans for the retreat after the attack. Jordan reflects on the fate which has brought him to this place. He thinks back to Madrid—he will take Maria there—and to all that he has learnt there about the war, its politics and its personalities. Especially he thinks of Gaylord's, the Russian headquarters, and of the Russian journalist Karkov who became a trusted friend. He compares this war with the American Civil War in which his grandfather fought. In the Spanish war the commanders of the International Brigades are virtually under Russian orders; and he thinks of the contrast between the idealism of the men in the Brigades and the cynical but realistic attitudes of their Russian Communist masters. These contrasts, and all that he has learnt about politics and war and people, are things he must write about honestly and clearly when the war is over.

NOTES AND GLOSSARY:

calliope: a fairground steam organ
elliptical: oval shaped
a kindergarten project: exercise in a school for small children
Keep off the wheel: Do not quarrel with Pablo and once more lose his collaboration. A reference to the wheel of fortune image which Hemingway has used at the beginning of the chapter
Grant: General Ulysses J. Grant (1822-85), who fought on the Northern or Union side in the American Civil War
Mantequerias Leonesas: a Madrid grocery store
Gran Via: one of the principal streets of Madrid
Gaylord's: hotel which housed the Russian delegation
Karkov: a Russian journalist; this character is based on Koltsov, the Pravda correspondent
Comintern: the Third Communist International, which provided help for the Spanish Republicans
Spanish Foreign Legion: military unit in Spanish Morocco, comprising mercenary soldiers of many nationalities under the command of Spanish officers
Abd el Krim: leader of the Riff rebellion in Spanish Morocco in 1921
Puerto de Santa Maria: town near Cadiz in south-west Spain
Berlitz School: famous language School with branches in most European countries
the Marx Brothers at the opera: *A Night at the Opera,* starring the Marx Brothers, was one of the outstanding Hollywood comedy films of the 1930s
Fuente Ovejuna: play of Lope de Vega's on the theme of the respect due to virtuous men

something wrong with Kashkin: he had disgraced himself or was politically suspect, and was 'working it out' or making amends by his service in Spain

porte-cochère: *(French)* covered entrance approached by carriage or car

the bubble reputation in the cannon's mouth: a punning allusion to Shakespeare's *As You Like It,* Act II scene vii and to John Keats's wine-cup (in his poem 'Ode to a Nightingale') 'with beaded bubbles winking at the brim'

Quantrills: William Quantrill operated as a raider or guerilla behind the lines in the American Civil War

Mosbys: John Mosby, another noted raider on the Southern or Confederate side in the Civil War

bushwhackers: ordinary guerilla soldiers, not the famous leaders

Vicksburg: on the Mississippi, where Grant beat the Confederate army in a famous battle

Sherman . . . McClellan: William Tecumseh Sherman (1820-91) and George Brinton McClellan (1826-85) were famous American Generals in the Civil War

Kleber, Lucasz, Hans (Kahle): commanders of the International Brigades

Guadalajara: where the Republicans won an outstanding victory over an army largely composed of Italian troops lent to the Nationalists by Mussolini

Bach: Johann Sebastian Bach (1685-1750), the famous German composer

Chartres Cathedral: fifty kilometres west of Paris, one of the greatest of medieval cathedrals

León: capital of the province of that name, with a superb Gothic cathedral

Mantegna: Andrea Mantegna (1431-1506), Italian painter

Greco: El Greco (1541-1614), Spanish painter, called El Greco because of his Greek origin

Breughel: Pieter Breughel (*c.*1520-69), Flemish painter

the Prado: national museum of paintings in Madrid

the Sanitarium: a hospital

Irun, San Sebastian, Vitoria: towns in north-eastern Spain

Carabanchel . . . Usera: on the outskirts of Madrid

the Tercio: the Third Regiment

does it smell like bitter almonds . . .?: it, cyanide poison

helmet like a football player's: the reference is to American football

Chesterfields: a brand of American cigarette

Puente de Toledo: the Toledo Bridge

the Alcazar: the palace, whose garrison held out against the Republicans during a prolonged siege. Karkov is being sarcastic about the British economist

gueule de conspirateur: (French) conspirator's face, mask, mug

dialectics: logical testing of truth; here used of Marxist political philosophy

Calvo Sotelo: Royalist member of the Spanish Parliament, whose murder was one of the incidents leading to the Civil War

Bukharin . . .: leading Soviet politicians condemned to death during Stalin's purges in the later 1930s

Mundo Obrero: *(Spanish)* literally *Workers' World;* the Spanish Communist newspaper

Modesto . . .: commanders of Republican army units

POUM: a Trotskyite Communist splinter-group

putsch: *(German)* political rising

Nin: Andrés Nin, POUM leader. Captured after the failure of the putsch, he seems to have been murdered, probably by a Stalinist agent

St Jean de Luz: town on the French side of the frontier, between San Sebastian and Bayonne

Burgos: capital of the Spanish kingdom of León and Castile

Upstairs people: the leaders, the top people

Borrow: George Borrow (1803-81), English writer, traveller and student of gypsy life, author of *The Bible in Spain* (1843)

Ford: Richard Ford (1796-1858), English author of *A Handbook for Travellers in Spain* (1845)

Chapter 19

In the course of conversation Pilar reveals to the band that it was Jordan who shot Kashkin. They discuss Kashkin's anxiety and premonition of his fate. Andrés asks if Jordan believes men can foresee their future, and Jordan dismisses the idea as superstition: Kashkin was afraid and let his fear become an obsession. Pilar says she saw death clearly marked on Kashkin's face, and speaks of the smell of death that hung around a certain bull-fighter in the hours before he was killed in the bull-ring. Jordan believes that such tales are made up by people after the events. Pilar gives further examples of men who had the smell of death on them, describing in disgusting terms the associations of the odour. Jordan relieves the oppressive atmosphere by joking that it was as well that he had put an end to

Kashkin if he smelt so bad. Looking out of the cave he sees that the snow has stopped: El Sordo's horses will leave tracks on its surface, he thinks.

NOTES AND GLOSSARY:

Qué cosa mas rara:	*(Spanish)* What a very strange business
De la muerte:	*(Spanish)* Of death
peon de brega:	*(Spanish)* torero who works on foot under the matador's orders during the early part of the bullfight
paseo:	*(Spanish)* formal entry of the bullfighters into the ring
tendido:	*(Spanish)* section of seats in the bull-ring
Plaza de Toros:	*(Spanish)* bull-ring
estribo, barrera:	*(Spanish)* the *barrera* is a wooden fence surrounding the arena. The *estribo* is a ledge about eighteen inches above ground level on the fence, to help the matadors to jump over the *barrera*
Leche:	*(Spanish)* milk (here, a swear-word)
cornada:	*(Spanish)* wound from a bull's horn
matadero:	*(Spanish)* slaughter-house
Manzanares:	river rising in the Sierra de Guadarrama
casas de putas:	*(Spanish)* brothels
Jardín Botánico:	*(Spanish)* the Botanic Gardens
gunny sack:	sack of coarse jute

Chapter 20

Jordan makes up his bed outside the cave, leaving his packs with Pilar. As he waits for Maria he turns from the memory of Pilar's talk about the smell of death to thoughts of clean pleasant smells which evoke his past life. Maria joins him. Like a bride she is wearing, she says, her wedding night-shirt. They make love and fall asleep; but Jordan wakes, feeling as if Maria were his whole life and that this is being taken away from him. He lies awake with his thoughts.

NOTES AND GLOSSARY:

Buenas noches:	*(Spanish)* Good night
I will respond:	I shall answer for, be responsible for. An example of Hemingway's anglicising of a Spanish idiom
sage:	sage-brush, a shrub which grows in desert country in the American West
Missoula:	town in western Montana, USA

Jonathan apple: a variety of dessert eating apple
cider mill: mill for crushing apples to extract the juice for making cider, an alcoholic drink
Como tu: *(Spanish)* like you; just as you are

Chapter 21

In the morning the snow is melting. Jordan hears a horse approaching. It is ridden by a Fascist cavalryman on patrol. Jordan shoots him and Primitivo captures the horse. Jordan is afraid that the rest of the cavalry troop will eventually follow the horse's tracks to the camp. Pablo says he will ride the horse round about to mislead the enemy. Jordan gives instructions to prepare to leave the camp and starts to take the machine gun to a position where it can defend the camp. Maria wants to go with him but he is concentrating only on the military situation.

NOTES AND GLOSSARY:
Thou hast much head: you are being very intelligent
bota: *(Spanish)* leather wine-skin
Que caballo mas bonito . . . mas hermoso: (Spanish) What a very pretty horse . . . beautiful horse
Thou to look after: a representation of a Spanish imperative construction

Chapter 22

Jordan sites the machine gun with the help of Primitivo, Agustín and Anselmo, hiding it from aircraft under pine branches. He reflects on the situation. There are not enough horses for the escape. Rafael appears, carrying two hares he has caught. Jordan is angry with him for having left his sentry-post and so let the enemy cavalryman through. The gypsy is likeable but totally unreliable. Jordan explains that they must try to avoid a fight with the cavalry troop if possible: their main object is to lie low till next day, when they must destroy the enemy posts at the sawmill and the road-mender's hut below the bridge, and blow up the bridge. In that way only can they help to ensure the success of Golz's attack on Segovia.

NOTES AND GLOSSARY:
frig: play about
we can swing the whole show: we can make the action a success
spooking out: making tracks out, moving away
mucked off: gone away (indecent colloquialism)

hijo de la gran puta: (Spanish) son of the great whore
Rediós!:   *(Spanish)* damn and blast!
Que tio!:   *(Spanish)* What a fellow!
requeté: *(Spanish)* soldier in a Carlist regiment, raised to support the claim to the Spanish throne of the descendants of Don Carlos de Bourbon (1788-1855)
Anda!:   *(Spanish)* Go!
Menuda matanza!: (Spanish) a tiny slaughter

Chapter 23

Four enemy cavalrymen appear. They look at the ground where Pablo turned the horse and one points in Jordan's direction, but after a moment they follow the tracks into the forest. Then a column of twenty cavalry goes past. Jordan is glad he did not have to shoot at the first four, as this would have brought the entire troop to the attack. It is clear that the machine gun is well hidden by the pine branches. Anselmo offers to go to La Granja to collect information. They discuss politics: they all want to fight to restore the Republican government, but not for anarchists and Communists. Agustín regrets that they did not kill the enemy.

NOTES AND GLOSSARY:
pommel: top of the arched front of a saddle
further forestal improvement: more trees to camouflage the gun. By using 'officialese' jokingly Jordan releases tension after the danger
Do men catch a wise stag without hounds?: a proverb referring to Pablo's skill when pursued
the quantity of dung he ate: the heap of insults he accepted
carajo: *(Spanish)* literally and figuratively, cock-up, debacle
the new religion: Christianity
Auto de Fé: sentence pronounced by the Spanish Inquisition, an ecclesiastical body set up in 1479 with Papal approval for the trial of heretics, and finally abolished in 1820

Chapter 24

The snow has almost gone as they breakfast and joke with one another. In more serious mood Agustín discloses that he also loves Maria. He tells Jordan to treat her with respect, for she is a girl of good morals and her sleeping with Jordan was not a casual or meaningless act. Jordan explains that he and Maria have had to do without the formality of marriage as they have so little time and must live out their lives together at once. Agustín trusts Jordan. He says all the band are to be trusted except the gypsy and Pablo. They hear shooting in the distance: it must be at El Sordo's. Agustín wants them to go and help El Sordo, but Jordan says they must stay where they are.

NOTES AND GLOSSARY:

Mighty like the rose. A rose is a rose is an onion: the first phrase is from an American popular song of the 1930s, the second is a parody of a well-known line by the American authoress Gertrude Stein. Agustín's reply shows that he does not understand Jordan's private world of literary reference

Stein: German for *stone* and pun on Gertrude Stein's surname

Carmelites: a twelfth century monastic order, whose female order dates from the fifteenth century. The Spanish Carmelite nuns, founded in 1562, were bound to especially strict disciplinary rules

joder: (Spanish) to copulate

Qué pasa?: (Spanish) What's happening?

Chapter 25

Jordan climbs up to Primitivo's sentry post. It is clear that El Sordo is under heavy fire. Primitivo wants to go to his aid but Jordan says it is useless, for they would all be killed. They must fight next day at the bridge. Pilar arrives and supports Jordan's arguments. An enemy plane flies over—a bad omen, says Pilar. It is bound to see El Sordo's position. Jordan tells Pilar to keep Maria in the cave if any aircraft fly overhead. Pilar goes to prepare food.

NOTES AND GLOSSARY:

Pobre: (Spanish) poor

jodido: (Spanish) done for (obscene, from *joder*)

an entire novel of dung: a long tale of obscenity

locos: (Spanish) lunatics

bad luck bird: Pilar likens the plane to a bird of ill omen

puchero: (Spanish) stew

physic: medicine

Chapter 26

Jordan examines the papers found on the dead cavalryman. There are letters from the man's family and from his fiancée: Jordan can not bear to read further. He reflects on death and the number of people he has killed in the war. The moral issues disturb him, and he knows he should not dwell on them because he must remain calm and resolute for the attack on the bridge. He has had to suppress some of his beliefs until the war is over. Then he hears many planes flying toward El Sordo's camp.

NOTES AND GLOSSARY:

Tafalla: town in north-east Spain about thirty kilometres from Pamplona

Marxist: follower of the theories of Karl Marx (1818-83) and his belief in international socialism

Liberty, Equality and Fraternity: slogan of the French Revolution which began in 1789

Life, Liberty and the Pursuit of Happiness: phrase in the Declaration of Independence which signalled the beginning of the American Revolution in 1776

Chapter 27

El Sordo is dug in on a hilltop surrounded by enemy troops. He has ridden there with four of his men. They have shot their horses so that their bodies plug gaps between rocks forming a defensive ring on the hilltop. Joaquín, the youngest, repeats Communist slogans but the others are cynical about Communist propaganda. El Sordo reflects on their situation: they have beaten off one attack by shooting and throwing hand grenades, but he knows they will be destroyed either by mortar shells or by aircraft bombs. He shoots five times into the ground to suggest that he and his men have committed suicide: then they reload and wait in silence. The cavalry Captain shouts obscene insults at them. He thinks they are dead and orders one of his men to go up and look. The soldier refuses and is defended by Lieutenant Berrendo, who despises the Captain as a cowardly bully whose orders have already caused the unnecessary deaths of his fellow Lieutenant and several of their men. Eventually the Captain goes up alone and El Sordo with grim humour shoots him. Then the planes come: ironically, El Sordo, being deaf, has not heard them but Joaquín points to them. El Sordo balances his gun on Joaquín's shoulder and fires at the planes while Joaquín, in terror, abandons his political slogans and prays to the Virgin Mary. The bombs fall, killing them all except Joaquín, who is unconscious and dying. Berrendo shoots him as an act of mercy. Berrendo looks at the dead on both sides. The bodies of his men are to be tied across the saddles of their horses. Then he reluctantly orders the heads of the 'bandits' (El Sordo's guerillas) to be cut off. He walks away, sickened by the brutality which war brings to all men.

NOTES AND GLOSSARY:

Mierda:	*(Spanish)* excrement (here used as a swear word)
Pasionaria:	the name adopted by the Moscow-trained Spanish Communist woman Dolores Ibarruri, whose impassioned speeches had great effect on Republican supporters in the Civil War
chancre:	venereal ulcer
trench mortar:	short portable cannon which fires shells at high angles
flayed:	skinned
me cago en tal:	*(Spanish)* to hell with it (obscene, *cagar* = to defecate)
he almost dove:	American past participle, English *dived*
canaille:	*(French)* mob, rabble
crupper:	hind quarters of a horse
caza mayor:	*(Spanish)* big game (of hunting)

Chapter 28

Jordan and Primitivo have heard the bombing, followed by the sound of further machine-gun fire and hand grenades thrown by Berrendo's troops to make sure El Sordo's men are all dead. At first Jordan thinks they may still be alive and holding on, but soon he realises all is over. Maria brings food as they speak of El Sordo's last fight. Primitivo feels they should have gone to his aid, but Jordan repeats that it would have been useless. Jordan sees Berrendo's troops ride past in the distance. They pass Anselmo who recognises El Sordo's rifle tied to a strangely shaped bundle on one of the horses. Going back to report to Jordan, he finds the bodies of El Sordo's men and realises that the bundle contained their heads. At the camp he learns that Pablo has already returned with news of the atrocity.

NOTES AND GLOSSARY:

She is giving me instruction: the word has a technical sense when converts are given instruction by a priest before being received into the Catholic Church: here Pilar's instruction is marital and sexual

'Hail, holy queen' . . .: Berrendo, like Joaquín and later in this chapter Anselmo, prays to the Virgin Mary after the day's brutality

Chapter 29

Jordan listens to Anselmo's report on the troop movements he has seen on the road, including Berrendo's cavalrymen. He decides to send Andrés through the lines to Golz's headquarters with a despatch which will make it clear that the attack should be called off in view of the enemy's preparations. If it is not called off he must still blow up the bridge. Pablo interrupts Jordan to say that he is confident they can destroy the bridge even without El Sordo's help.

NOTES AND GLOSSARY:
were officers by their sleeves: had officers' badges on their uniforms
Estado Mayor: (Spanish) headquarters of the Divisional Staff
SIM: Military Intelligence Service

Chapter 30

Jordan reflects that Golz will probably not be able to cancel the attack since he will have to wait for authorisation from his superiors in Madrid, whose previous tactical mistakes Jordan recalls. He must keep his nerve for the attack on the bridge, though he has been shaken by the beheading of El Sordo's band. He reflects on his boyhood interest in military history, fostered by his grandfather's account of his service in the American Civil War. His grandfather, who survived four years of war, had seen men scalped by the Indians. He recalls his grandfather's cavalry sword and pistol: his father had later committed suicide with this pistol. Thoughts of his grandfather are a comfort to Jordan, who finds it difficult to focus his thoughts calmly on his father. He recalls what his grandfather had told him about the American Civil War and the character of its leaders. He finds it ironic, in his present circumstances, that his grandfather, an American Republican, would have nothing to do with members of the Democratic party in the United States. His thoughts are disturbed and he controls them by imagining the results if Golz's attack should prove successful. He is suddenly convinced that he will have to blow up the bridge, and this certainty in its own way calms his nerves.

NOTES AND GLOSSARY:
Soria: town about two hundred kilometres north-east of Madrid

Siguenza:	town about one hundred and ten kilometres north-east of Madrid, a Nationalist stronghold
Arganda:	on the main road from Madrid eastwards to Valencia
Durán:	a commander in the International Brigades
Smith and Wesson:	an American firm of pistol manufacturers
coroner:	official appointed to enquire into mysterious or violent deaths
Custer:	George Armstrong Custer (1839-76) an American General who fought in the Civil War and afterwards in campaigns against the Indians. Defeated in his famous 'last stand' against the Sioux at Little Big Horn in Montana
Lache:	*(French)* coward
snotty:	(slang) proud, superior
Anheuser-Busch lithograph:	engraved print published by this American brewery company
Phil Sheridan . . . .:	Civil War commanders: see note on Chapter 18
Democrat:	member of the Democratic Party (USA)
clochards:	*(French)* down-and-outs, tramps
Quatorzième Brigade:	*(French)* 14th International Brigade

Chapter 31

That night Jordan and Maria, in the sleeping-bag, do not make love since Maria is in pain. They talk of going to Madrid, of what they will do there, and of marriage. Maria confesses that Pilar has said they will all die next day. Jordan, though he feels afraid, dismisses the idea as rubbish. Again they talk of life together in Madrid and Maria speaks of Pilar's instructions about a wife's duties. She then recounts the story of how her parents were shot by the Fascists and her own ordeal when her head was shaved and she was repeatedly raped. She is afraid she may not be able to have children and that Jordan will not want to marry her. He comforts her, saying they are already man and wife and truly married. He is proud of Maria and of her family.

NOTES AND GLOSSARY:

Onan:	see the Bible, *Genesis,* Chapter 38 for this reference to masturbation
Seguridad:	*(Spanish)* the Security office
manure:	euphemism for an indecent expression in Spanish
As Garbo:	see note on Chapter 11: Maria here expresses the image in Jordan's earlier private fantasies
armoire:	*(French)* wardrobe

. . . y vivan mis padres!: (Spanish) and long live my parents!

Falangist:	member of the Falange, the Spanish Fascist Party
Red nuns . . .:	novices have their heads shaven on becoming nuns and 'brides of Christ': the Falangist is mocking women who embrace the Communist cause
UHP:	*Union de Hijos del Pueblo:* the Union of Daughters of the People, a Republican women's organisation; but translated as *una hija de puta* (daughter of a whore) by the Falangist troops, who painted the slogan on the foreheads of Republican women prisoners
Cortez . . .:	Cortez, Pizarro, notoriously cruel sixteenth century conquerors of Mexico and Peru; Menedez de Aviles (not Avila) massacred the French and established the Spanish in Florida; Lister, see note on Chapter 15
the reformation:	religious movement which broke away from Rome in sixteenth century to found the Protestant Churches

Chapter 32

At Gaylord's in Madrid Karkov joins a gathering of Communist political and military leaders and propagandists. There is much gossip. There is talk of Golz's offensive, indicating a security leak. It is also rumoured that the Fascists are fighting amongst themselves. A General is angry about the gossip. Karkov is planning to set off for Golz's headquarters at 2 a.m.

NOTES AND GLOSSARY:

calcimine:	a lime solution, whitewash
Dolores . . .:	la Pasionaria and other political figures are referred to here
Izvestia:	an official Soviet Russian newspaper
lead:	opening paragraph of a newspaper story
a Hungarian:	the reference is probably to General Gall, or perhaps to General Kleber, of the International Brigades
függler:	probably in the sense of opportunist, conspirator

Chapter 33

At 2 a.m. Pilar wakes Jordan to tell him that Pablo has gone: he has slit open Jordan's packs and stolen some dynamite and, worse still, detonators, fuse, and the firing device. Two of the horses are missing. Pilar is ashamed of her failure to guard the packs and angry at Pablo's treachery. Jordan controls his own anger and assures Pilar that he can improvise some means of exploding the dynamite at the bridge.

NOTES AND GLOSSARY:

as cocked as the pistol: as tensely ready for action as a pistol that has been cocked and is ready to fire

Chapter 34

Andrés, carrying Jordan's despatch to Golz, makes his way past the Fascist posts towards the Republican lines. As a peasant, his regrets on the wastefulness of war are focused on the abandoned hay crops in the fields. He feels reprieved by being sent away from danger with the message for Golz. He thinks back to his boyhood when, although he felt afraid, he won a reputation for bravery at the annual bull-baiting in his village. Reflecting that, once he has delivered the despatch, he must return to help his brother Eladio and the rest of the partizans in the attack on the bridge, he reaches the lines.

NOTES AND GLOSSARY:

set-gun: gun set with blank charge to give warning when triggered

haycocks: heaps of hay drying in the fields before being carried to the farmyard

bull-baiting: sport in which a bull is teased into angry attacks

Villaconejos: the name of Andrés's village

use them for callers: to attract wild partridges by their cries

crayfish: shellfish like a small lobster, here a freshwater variety

Chapter 35

Jordan lies beside Maria who is still asleep. In his thoughts he gives vent to his anger with Pablo and accuses Spain of a whole history of treachery. His rage subsides, and speaking softly and calmly, he says they will all die at the bridge and that his wedding gift to Maria has been not to disturb her last night's sleep.

NOTES AND GLOSSARY:

mucked: euphemism for an obscenity

like a damned wailing wall: reference to the wall of Jewish ritual lamentation in Jerusalem

Largo:	Largo Caballero, Republican political leader who headed the coalition of left-wing parties
Prieto:	see note on Chapter 13
Asensio:	a Republican War Minister dismissed under Communist pressure
Miaja, Rojo:	Republican Generals defending Madrid
Pablo Iglesias:	outstanding Spanish Socialist reformer
Durutti:	Anarchist leader, killed probably by one of his own followers
Kleber:	see note on Chapter 18
what he would have to do:	that is, an improvised method of blowing up the bridge

---

Chapter 36

Andrés is challenged by the Republican troops, who suspect he is a spy. There is a humorous exchange, but the confusion, inefficiency and lack of discipline of the soldiers is clearly demonstrated. At last Andrés is allowed to enter the trenches and finds that the soldiers are Anarchists. Their leader wastes more time over the examination of his papers but eventually agrees to take him to his Commanding Officer.

NOTES AND GLOSSARY:

Salud, milicianos!: (Spanish) Hullo, militiamen!; Hey, soldiers!

Quiero decir, que buena alambrada: (Spanish) I mean to say, what good wire

God in a latrine:	presumably a current blasphemy
FAI:	Anarchist Secret Society
CNT:	the Anarcho-Syndicalist Trade Union
bodega:	*(Spanish)* wine-vault
Aranjuez:	town fifty kilometres south of Madrid
Villacastin:	town near Segovia
tomate:	*(Spanish)* tomato, spilling of blood
carabine:	*(Spanish)* rifle

Chapter 37

Jordan lies awake, checking on the time. He embraces Maria who wakes up: they make love and again experience ecstasy. As they dress and prepare for the day ahead of them, Jordan reflects that he has learnt more about life in the past four days than in all the time before.

NOTES AND GLOSSARY:

| marten: | a small weasel-like animal, much prized for its fur |

lance-pointed, luminous splinter: note how throughout this paragraph the movement of the minute-hand of the watch is also an image of the movement of Jordan's sexual desire

Then they were together . . .: another passage of poetic lyricism in describing the experience of love and sexual union. See note on passage in Chapter 7

la gloria: (Spanish) the mystical ecstasy of the soul

Cante Hondo: style of Andalusian gypsy song

Saetas: songs addressed to the Virgin Mary

San Juan de la Cruz: St John of the Cross, sixteenth century Spanish mystical poet

Charles, Chub, . . .: Jordan recalls the names of friends: they do not figure in the novel

---

Chapter 38

In the cave they eat and prepare their equipment. There is much tension between them. Jordan now realises that without Pablo they have not enough people to be certain of destroying both the enemy posts, at the sawmill above and the road-mender's hut below the bridge. The operation seems headed for disaster. He tells himself he must show greater confidence. He talks to Pilar, who says Maria should stay in safety holding the horses while she herself will take on Pablo's duties and attack the lower post. She also tells Jordan that she had been talking gypsy nonsense about reading his fate in his hand: he is not to worry about it, and all will be well. She declares her affection for him. Suddenly Pablo reappears. He says he has recruited five more men. He has thrown away the equipment he stole from Jordan; but his moment of weakness has passed and he has come back to fight with them. He tells Jordan that he has worked out a method of detonating the dynamite with a hand-grenade. So has Jordan, who is relieved by the turn of events. Pablo speaks to Pilar, explaining that the men he has brought think that he is the leader of the band. Pilar restores him to that role: she is moved to find that he is once again a man of courage and action.

NOTES AND GLOSSARY:

Mills bomb: type of hand-grenade named after its inventor

cotter pin: a pin which holds a mechanism in place

Valen más que pesan: (Spanish) they are worth more than they weigh

a political commissar: Jordan turns Pilar's words of comfort into a shared ironic joke

Ni tu, ni Dios: (Spanish) neither you nor God

Canst thou spit?:	fear has the effect of drying up the saliva in one's mouth
Qué mal lo pasé!:	*(Spanish)* How badly I spent it!; What a bad time I had!
Judas Iscariot:	the disciple who betrayed Christ; the archetype of the traitor

Chapter 39

As they climb the hill with their laden horses Pablo tells Jordan that the men he has brought expect the operation to be successful: their morale must be kept up. Their horses will be held with the others during the action. Pablo will attack the lower post with the five men, then fall back on the bridge. He thinks they have a good chance of escaping to Gredos. Jordan reflects on the situation. His confidence is returning and he is indifferent to the possibility of failure and death. They meet the waiting men. Jordan notices that one of them is riding the gray horse belonging to the dead cavalryman. Pablo leads the way to where they will leave the horses.

NOTES AND GLOSSARY:

conversion on the road to Tarsus: Jordan's ironic reference is to the conversion of St Paul to Christianity: Pablo is the Spanish form of Paul

canonising you: declaring you to be a Saint

another flash . . . revelation: as St Paul had, see note above

a schizophrenic: in medical terms, one whose intellectual and emotional processes are dissociated and at odds

Rafael will be with thee: notice that Jordan keeps the unreliable gypsy out of the attack

Que me maten: *(Spanish)* Strike me dead

Chapter 40

Andrés continues to make slow progress towards Golz's headquarters. After the anarchist officer he meets the battalion commander, Gomez, who decides to take him personally on a motor-cycle to brigade headquarters. There, after further obstruction, they get through to a professional army officer, a Lieutenant-Colonel who issues them with a new safe-conduct pass and sends them onwards.

NOTES AND GLOSSARY:

guerrillero: *(Spanish)* guerilla, partizan

Teniente-Coronel: *(Spanish)* Lieutenant-Colonel

epsom salts: magnesium sulphate, used as a purgative medicine
I always shaved myself . . .: the officer continues to insult Gomez as a
                former barber
sodium bicarbonate: alkaline powder used to correct bad digestion
milicianas: *(Spanish)* women soldiers
Salvoconducto: *(Spanish)* safe-conduct pass
use your lights: the army vehicles concealed their movements by
                driving without headlamps
Pequerinos: a battle early in the Civil War
forking the motor: sitting with legs astride the motor-cycle

Chapter 41

Pablo, Jordan and the band reach the place where they are to leave the
horses. Jordan repeats that no-one is to shoot until they hear the
sound of the bombs which will mean that Golz's attack has begun.
Pablo prepares to leave for the lower post. He says quietly to Jordan
that although there is a shortage of horses, there will be one for
Jordan. Jordan lays aside his suspicions about the meaning of this
remark. Pablo and Jordan wish each other luck and Pablo departs.
Jordan briefly says goodbye to Maria. He feels as if he were watching
a train take away those he loves, and he recalls the sentimental goodbye of his father when he, Jordan, was going off as a boy to boarding-
school for the first time. Jordan takes Anselmo and Agustín down
through the pine-forest to place the machine-gun in position so as to
cover Pablo's retreat and the attack on the sentries at the bridge. He
goes over the final plan. Jordan and Anselmo are to shoot the sentries
while Agustín covers them: Jordan is then to fix the explosive charges
to the bridge, wire them up, and stand by in readiness to blow up the
bridge. As he checks the final details with Anselmo, he thinks again of
his father: Jordan is himself in a protective fatherly role in relation to
the brave, simple old peasant. Then he settles down to wait.

NOTES AND GLOSSARY:
hobble: to tie the legs of a horse loosely so that it will not
                wander
Do not molest me more: Spanish idiom: 'do not go on at me'
De la primera: *(Spanish)* literally 'of the first (quality)'; perfect,
                fine
Off the top of the basket: an extended allusion to the preceding
                phrase. Market traders put the best of their fruit
                on the top of the basket to attract customers
Suerte: *(Spanish)* Good luck
reptilian: like a snake or lizard, cold, scaly and repulsive

au fond:	*(French)* at bottom, basically
equivocation:	misunderstanding, mistake
sage hens:	species of American game bird found in sage-brush country, see note on Chapter 20
was crouched on his haunches:	defecating. Hemingway wishes to emphasise the comically solemn formality of Fernando's manners
de acuerdo?:	*(Spanish)* understood?
pull-through:	cleaning-rag for the barrel of a gun
Robert Jordan lay . . .:	In the construction of the novel Hemingway picks up the same descriptive pattern for this paragraph as he used when introducing the hero in this setting in Chapter 1
shucked:	a homely metaphor, from shelling peas from the pea-pod

Chapter 42

Andrés and Gomez make good progress in spite of being held up by a traffic block. Andrés is deeply impressed by the lorryloads of Republican troops on the move. At a command post Gomez asks for directions to Golz's headquarters. A staff car arrives with officers of the International Brigades including a French Communist Political Commissar, André Massart*, whom Gomez recognises. He asks Massart to direct him to Golz. Gomez does not know that Massart has become mentally unbalanced with vanity, jealousy and suspicion of political intrigues. Massart takes Jordan's despatch and the safe-conduct pass and orders the arrest of Gomez and Andrés. The guard tells Gomez that Massart is insane and promises to report the incident to the first responsible officer he sees. Eventually Massart interrogates his two prisoners. Gomez expostulates with him. Massart leaps to the conclusion that they are Fascists and that Golz is in league with them: in his crazed mind he elaborates his suspicions that Golz is a traitor. He orders the guard to lock up Gomez and Andrés. Massart ponders over his suspicions and the action he should take. Finally Karkov enters with two other Russians. He has been told of the arrest by the guard and has ordered the release of the prisoners. Karkov is politely insulting to Massart. He recovers the despatch and other papers and sends Gomez and Andrés onwards. Karkov threatens to bring political pressure against Massart. Gomez and Andrés deliver Jordan's despatch. Duval, Golz's Chief of Staff, reads it and decides the attack should be cancelled. By the time he contacts Golz, who is visiting a forward observation post, it is too late: the bombers are already flying

*In TP his name is given as Marty.

overhead. Golz accepts the situation stoically. Once more a well-planned, and on this occasion well-equipped, attack has been doomed to failure by political treachery and by lack of discipline. Ironically, this attack has hardly yet been launched.

NOTES AND GLOSSARY:

klaxon: electric motor-car horn

differential: gear wheels transmitting motion to the axles

casques: *(French)* helmets

mucho, mucho: *(Spanish)* great, super

Comandancia: *(Spanish)* command post, command HQ

chasseurs à pied: *(French)* French light infantry

comrade Massart: the character is based on André Marty, one of the International Brigade commanders

Aspesar de eso, esta loco: (Spanish) In spite of that, he's crazy

Como lo oyes: *(Spanish)* Like you heard

Divagationers: *(Spanish)* people who do not follow the official party line

Tiene mania de fusilar gente: (Spanish) He's got an obsession about shooting people

Salvarsan: a drug used for treating syphilis

probity: honesty

defalcation: embezzlement, misappropriation of funds

close to Tukachevsky: a friend of Tukachevsky, Russian Field-Marshal put to death by Stalin in 1937 for allegedly conspiring with Germany

Voroshilov: Klimenti Efremonich Voroshilov (1881-1969), Russian Field-Marshal, supporter of Stalin's purges in the 1930s

Gall: Hungarian who became a Soviet citizen and commanded in the International Brigades

Putz: one of the International Brigade commanders

Me cago en su puta madre!: (Spanish) I shit on his whore of a mother

mimeographed copy: duplicated from a type-written stencil

It is doubtful if . . .: In this paragraph Hemingway breaks the fictional structure of his novel by intervening with a personal comment on the situation and on military operations in general

Tovarich: *(Russian)* Comrade

gunner's mate: naval gunnery petty officer

chief yeoman, first-class yeoman: the former is a petty officer, the latter a trained 'rating', or sailor, in the naval signals branch

Pravda: official newspaper of the Soviet government

Azerbaijan: republic in the Soviet Union, in Transcaucasia
Et maintenant fiche-moi la paix: (French) and now leave me in peace
position Segovia . . . Avila: not the cities. Golz has used these as
          code-names for his various military units
Nous sommes foutus: (French) We're scuppered; we're done for
Comme toujours . . . c'est dommage: (French) As always . . . it's a
          pity
Black Sea . . . Alicante: Golz traces the sea-route from the USSR to
          the Spanish port of discharge
balls up: confusion, disaster (indecent)
Rien à faire . . .: *(French)* There's nothing to be done. Nothing.
          Don't let's think about it. We've just got to take it
Bon. Nous ferons notre petit possible: (French) Right. We'll do
          whatever we can

Chapter 43

Jordan watches the sentries at the bridge as the new day dawns. His
mind is filled with thoughts of Andrés, Golz and the progress of the
war; with keeping a close watch on the sentries; and with the sights,
sounds and smells of the natural scenery around him. Suddenly he
hears bombs falling in the distance. He shoots one sentry, Anselmo
shoots the other. There is the sound of hand-grenades and rifle-fire
from the lower post which Pablo and his five men are attacking and
from the sawmill above, under attack from Pilar and the rest of the
band. Jordan and Anselmo tie the explosive charges to the iron girders
of the bridge. As they work Jordan listens to the firing and tries to
interpret what is happening. He runs a wire from his improvised firing
device to the roadside and shows Anselmo how to use it. Pilar's party
returns from the sawmill: Eladio is missing and Fernando badly
wounded. Jordan tells Anselmo to blow up the bridge if a tank or
armoured car comes on to it. He returns to fix the wire to the charges
on the other side of the bridge. Fernando knows he is dying and asks
to be left with a rifle to cover the bridge. Anselmo reflects on death
and killing: he hopes to atone for killing the sentry. They hear fresh
firing from Pablo's direction and the new sound of a heavy machine
gun. As Jordan runs back across the bridge with the second wire an
enemy truck appears on the road above. They blow the bridge. Jordan
is unhurt but Anselmo is killed by a flying splinter of steel. Jordan
joins Pilar. Their initial bitterness about the death of their friends
soon passes and they concentrate on covering the road ·for Pablo's
return. They hear aircraft overhead.

     Maria is waiting with the horses. To control her nervousness as she
hears the shooting she tries to focus her thoughts on the realities of

Pablo and Pilar attacking the posts. She is praying confusedly for Jordan as she hears the bridge blown up. Then she hears Pilar shouting that Jordan is safe.

Enemy planes fly overhead: Pilar is afraid but Jordan says they are seeking a different target. Jordan joins Agustín. They hear several bursts of fire from Pablo's gun; then Pablo appears, firing inter-mittently behind him. A light tank is in pursuit but it retreats when Jordan fires. Pablo catches up with them as they return to the horses. He says his five recruits are dead: now there will be enough horses for the escape. Jordan and Agustín realise that Pablo has murdered his companions. Pablo starts to lead his band to safety. As they cross the road in single file the tank shells them. Jordan is the last to go. A heavy tank has arrived. Jordan's horse is hit and rolls on him, break-ing his left thigh-bone and crushing the nerve. Primitivo and Agustín pull him to safety. Jordan tells Pablo to leave him behind. Maria wants to stay with him but he says she must go. What he now must do, he must do alone; but they are now as one person; and wherever she goes, all that will remain of him will also go. Pilar and Pablo take the protesting Maria away. Agustín offers to shoot Jordan who says it is not necessary. As he waits for the end, alone and without even the comfort of his whisky flask, he tries to think calmly about his life and his beliefs. His leg starts to give pain, and he is tempted to shoot him-self but holds on, hoping to delay the enemy pursuit. Then he sees cavalry approaching, led by an officer who is Lieutenant Berrendo. Jordan lies on the pine-needles in the forest, waiting for Berrendo to come into close range in the sights of his sub-machine gun.

NOTES AND GLOSSARY:
portable short-wave sets: for radio communication
If I can spit by then: if my mouth is not dry with fear
Buena caza: *(Spanish)* Good shooting; nice hunting
Sin novedad: *(Spanish)* All quiet; all OK
like a bloody Tarzan in a rolled steel forest: a reference to Tarzan the ape-man, hero of the novels of Edgar Rice Bur-roughs and the films made from them in the 1920s and 1930s. Jordan ironically sees himself amid the girders of the bridge like Tarzan in the jungle
jelly: slang term for the explosive, gelignite
Anselmo got a cripple: he only crippled the sentry with his first shot, and had to shoot again to finish him off *(rematarlo =* to kill again)
the damned Jordan: the River Jordan. His thoughts, as so often in moments of tension, begin to jump from one association to another

As Maine goes so goes the nation: common phrase in election predictions in the USA

Israelites: the Old Testament tribes

inutile: useless

Like swallows . . . like wash boilers: Notice Pilar's reaction as opposed to Rafael's romantic simile

Vaya mandanga: *(Spanish)* Go on, slow-coach

Es muy concienzudo!: *(Spanish)* He is very thorough

as an outfielder goes backwards for a long fly ball: comparison from the game of baseball

culvert: large pipe or conduit to carry water under a road

TNT: trinitrotoluene, a high explosive

mierda: *(Spanish)* dung

Sigue tirando: *(Spanish)* Follow them as you fire

gentled: patted, stroked

cinch: saddle-girth

cocks in the pit: fighting-cocks in a cockpit or ring

brass hulls: cartridge-cases

flash-cone: guard around the barrel

the Fiat in that little tank: cannon made by the Fiat company

hackamore: halter

No hace falta: *(Spanish)* There is no need

a good spot of the giant-killer: a measure of whisky to kill his fears and deaden his pain

Ones with religion or just taking it straight?: those who believe in an after-life or those who believe only in the world they know

That's what it will be like: death

Part 3

Commentary

The moral theme

The quotation from John Donne (1572-1631) which Hemingway placed at the front of *For Whom The Bell Tolls*, and from which the title is taken, carries the message of the novel's underlying theme. No man is an island, entirely on his own. We are all connected, one with another, as members of the human race; and the fate that touches one individual touches all.

Hemingway clearly intended the quotation to be some kind of comment on his book. It is in fact an extract from a sermon. We are probably meant to regard it as a sort of text whose implications are worked out for us in the pages of the novel. As we have seen in the introductory study of his life and work, Hemingway returned to Spain as a war correspondent during the Civil War, and lent his support to the Republican cause both by his sympathetic reporting and by raising money to buy ambulances. The novel is in many ways a statement of his own sense of involvement. Though we should guard against confusing the personal opinions of the author of a novel with those of the characters whose behaviour and opinions are set out in his fiction, in Hemingway's case we can often find fairly close correspondences. This is true of the moral message contained in the Donne quotation and worked out in the person of Robert Jordan.

The echo of this message resounded in the ears of all perceptive observers of the political and economic scene in the 1930's. In Europe and America economic depression had led to high unemployment and political discontent. In some countries, notably Germany and Italy, totalitarian regimes had been established. These were becoming in their own ways as repressive of individual liberty internally as Stalin's regime was in the USSR. At the same time their leaders tried to divert attention from internal problems by aggressive moves against others, Mussolini with his imperialist adventures in Albania and Africa, Hitler first with his racial attacks on those who were not of pure 'Aryan' or Nordic descent, then later with his own imperialist adventures against other European countries. Western liberals could see that the values they believed in were everywhere being attacked and eroded. For politicians the solution lay in alliances of collective security, the application of John Donne's theme on the scale of individual nations. Artists and writers interpreted the theme on the level of the individual person. 'We must love one another and die' wrote the English poet W. H. Auden (1907-73).

Political attitudes

When the Spanish Civil War broke out, with a military and monarchist rebellion against an elected popular government, liberals in many countries responded by rallying to the support of the Republicans. Liberal democracy was threatened, and the cause of the Spanish people was that of all free people. Hence the International Brigades, led by Spanish and other Russian-trained Communist advisers and commissars, who were counter-balanced on Franco's side by German and Italian air force units and equipment.

Hemingway's own commitment to the political left wing, however, was very far from total. He demonstrates this in his novel in two ways.

Firstly, it is not only the Fascists whom he presents as violent and cruel—see for instance Chapter 31 when Maria tells Jordan how her parents were shot and how she herself was raped by the Fascists. He also presents episodes of equal cruelty on the part of the Republican loyalists; see Chapter 10 for Pilar's account of Pablo's attack on the Fascist officials in a provincial town '. . . the worst day of my life until . . . three days later when the fascists took the town'. Again he shows that many of the Communist political commissars were corrupt and inefficient. Jordan contrasts the idealism of the volunteers in the Brigades with the cynicism of their Russian-trained masters (Chapter 18); the French Political Commissar Massart interferes by ordering the arrest of Andrés on his way to warn Golz to cancel the attack (Chapter 42).

Secondly, he presents several of his characters as uncommitted to the Communists. In Chapter 23 members of the guerrilla band agree that they all want to fight to restore the Republic, but not for Communism and Anarchism; while in Chapter 26 Jordan thinks unhappily of the way he has had to suspend some of his own moral beliefs until the war is won: 'You're not a real Marxist and you know it.'

Students should read these passages carefully and try to memorise key quotations to be used in answering questions about the political attitudes portrayed in the novel. When it was published Hemingway was accused by some critics of being pro-Communist and by others of sympathising with the Fascists. What does this say about their respective attitudes and his own? Where do Hemingway's sympathies really lie? With the politicians? Or with the ordinary people of Spain? The answer seems to be that Hemingway himself was opposed to totalitarian rule from either the right or the left. He was for the liberty of the individual to act and think according to his own conscience, and sympathised especially with those who found themselves, like Jordan and Anselmo, forced to reply to violence with violence in order to establish a world in which gentleness and decency could survive. See for instance Chapter 23 when Anselmo says that no revenge should be taken on the Fascists after the war has been won, and Chapter 43 when he reflects on death and killing and hopes to atone for having shot the sentry.

Let us turn now from these considerations of the moral and political aspects of the novel, and examine it more closely as an example of Hemingway's literary art.

Heroes and the code

We have already discussed the values of the heroic code which Hemingway elaborates in his work. How are these values demonstrated in *For Whom The Bell Tolls*?

Jordan and the guerillas are all living under extreme pressure. The sabotage operation at the bridge is highly dangerous and it is unlikely that they will get away alive. We can begin by listing the characters who consistently respond to this pressure with grace and courage—notably Jordan, Pilar, Anselmo and El Sordo. They are all ready to sacrifice their lives selflessly for the cause, in contrast to the wavering response of Pablo, a complex character whose former virtues have begun to turn bad, and who will stoop to treachery in order to save his own skin.

Some minor characters

We should also consider some minor characters whose behaviour conforms to or deviates from the code. Golz is a code hero, self-reliant, ironic, realistic, especially in his acceptance of the failure of his attack (P.pp.392-3, TP.pp.375-6). Massart on the other hand, corrupted by 'disappointment, bitterness . . . and thwarted ambition' (P.p.381, TP.p.365), is the antithesis of the code hero. Where does the journalist, Karkov, stand in relation to the heroic code? He is a realist, cynical, powerful, decisive, especially in dealing with Massart's interference with Jordan's messenger (P.p.387, TP.p.370, onwards). He is also the man most responsible, through his cynical realism, for the completion of Jordan's political education at Gaylord's, where 'you learned how it was all really done instead of how it was supposed to be done' (P.p.216, TP.p.206, onwards). But the reader should consider Hemingway's ironic comment, after presenting Karkov deliberately telling a lie, that the one thing Karkov was never cynical about was his belief in the value of his own benevolent intervention (P.p.389, TP.p.372). Golz, Massart, and Karkov are all well worth studying both for their roles in the action and plot of the novel, and as minor examples of the way in which Hemingway projects conflicting moral values.

Robert Jordan

The main example of the Hemingway code hero is Robert Jordan. Brave, honest, and honourable, compassionate and tender, an intelligent and realistic appraiser of others and of himself, he is both a thinker and a man of action. In some ways his critical intelligence and imagination add to the pressures on him. When his thoughts about the operational problems facing him become uncomfortably tense he takes refuge in private linguistic games (P.p.258, TP.p.152), in sexual fantasies (P.p.130-1, TP.p.126), in the cure-all (P.p.50, TP.p.51) of alcohol, and in ironic joking, often to himself (see the chapter summaries for comment and explanation). But note that at the end he faces death without the aid of the 'giant-killer' (P.p.428, TP.p.409): Jordan is finally in command of himself, alone and unaided, despite the final extremity of the pressures he has endured. These have included witnessing the lynching of a negro when he was a child of seven (P.p.111, TP.pp.108-9), embarassment at his father's sentimental religiosity in their personal relationship (P.pp.371, TP.p.355), and especially shame at his father's suicide by means of the pistol his grandfather had used in the American Civil War (P.p.64, TP.p.65; P.p.310, TP.p.297). Jordan resists the temptation to shoot himself as he lies alone at the end, tortured with the pain of a broken leg (P.p.430-1, TP.p.411). He atones for his father's act and lives up to the standards of courage set by his grandfather.

In his relationship with Maria he is strong, protective, and tender. She has suffered terribly and is still psychologically disturbed (P.p.33, TP.p.35). Jordan's love wipes out the emotional scars left on her by her experiences: in the place of sexual violation there is tenderness and consideration, leading to the sexual communion and ecstasy Maria calls *la gloria*. Students should notice particularly the love scenes in Chapters 7, 13 and 37, and the way in which Maria's initial fear that Jordan will despise her is set at rest. Alone after her family had been murdered, she is now no longer alone even when Jordan stays behind to meet his death; nor is he alone at the end. As he puts it, 'I go always with thee wherever thou goest . . . Thou art me too now. Thou art all there will be of me.' (P.pp.424-5, TP.pp.405-6).

Finally, we should regard Jordan's intellectual honesty as another manifestation of the heroic code. It shows in his recognition of his own nervous tensions; in his thoughts about the political realities of the cause to which he is committed; and in his relations with the guerillas with whom he plans this dangerous operation. Consider especially his detached appreciation of the Spanish temperament (P.p.129, TP.p.125); his reasons for fighting in Spain and his independence of political propaganda (P.pp.153-7, TP.pp.147-51); and his troubled conscience about the number of people he has had to kill (P.pp.280-1, TP.p.268).

'You were fighting against exactly what you were doing and being forced into doing to have any chance of winning.' (P.p.153, TP.p.147)

'You have to put many things into abeyance to win a war.' (P.p.282, TP.p.269)

'Here in Spain the communists offered the best discipline and the soundest and sanest for the prosecution of the war,' but afterwards he would 'write a true book' about it (P.p.155, TP.p.149), as Hemingway himself tried to do in this many-sided novel.

Jordan and Maria: the sub-plot

Jordan's relationship with Maria constitutes a romantic sub-plot. As such, we would not expect Maria to sustain as important a part as some of the other characters. She is depicted in the traditionally submissive role of the female in Spanish society. Her desire is to serve her husband as Pilar has instructed her (P.p.161, TP.p.155): despite her traumatic past, she represents youth and innocence, in contrast to age and experience. Her first sexual encounter with Jordan shows this; she is ashamed and frightened (P.p.67, TP.p.67); she does not know how to kiss or 'where the noses go' (P.pp.68-9, TP.pp.68-9); she has to ask Jordan to help her since she does not know what she is expected to do (P.p.68, TP.p.68). Notice also her relationship with the young Joaquín at El Sordo's camp, full of the teasing (P.pp.125-6, TP.pp.121-3) and the sympathy (P.p.132, TP.p.128) one finds in sister and brother. Even at the end, when Jordan persuades her to go on with the rest of the band, we feel that she is still innocence swept onwards by forces greater than she understands.

The sub-plot fills more than one function, however. Besides offering idyllic romantic interludes in contrast with the main issues of war and violence, it enriches the texture of the relationships between Jordan and the other characters. This is true of even a minor character like Agustín, who tells Jordan to treat Maria with respect because she is a girl of good morals: their discussion and arrival at a mutual understanding cement Agustín's trust in Jordan and his conduct of the sabotage operation (P.pp.269-71, TP.pp.257-9). With the major characters, Pilar and Pablo, this function of the sub-plot is particularly important.

Pilar

The portrait of Pilar is magnificently drawn. She is the most—perhaps the only—fully developed example of a female code hero in Hemingway's work. Physically she is impressive, tall, strongly built, powerful. As a personality she is equally impressive. She dominates the guerilla band and plays the role of leader now that Pablo has lost his authority. The others all respect her, with a respect that includes a measure of fear of her stinging tongue. But she is also capable of great affection and tenderness. This has centred mainly on Maria, whom she has protected and nursed back into physical and mental health; and we see how she hands Maria on to Jordan to complete the therapy. Like all the code heroes, she has experience, self-knowledge, and emotional honesty. These show, for instance, in her recognition of one of the strands in the fabric of her relationship with Maria, who being inexperienced, fails fully to understand.

'I have never wanted thee . . . He can have thee, but I am jealous.'

Pilar's grasp of the complexity of human relationships is pointed up by her further paradoxical comments.

'I am no *tortillera* but a woman made for men . . . I do not make perversions. I only tell you something true. Few people will ever talk to thee truly and no women. I am jealous and say it and it is there. And I say it.' (P.p.147, TP.pp.141-2)

Pilar's relationship with Jordan demonstrates her knowledge, both physical and psychological, of men and their behaviour also. This is clear not only in her discussion of sexual matters, for example Pablo's impotence after the killings in the town (P.p.123, TP.p.119), and her rough teasing of Jordan:

'I am gross,' Pilar said. 'But I am also very delicate.' (P.p.149, TP.p.143).

She also understands the precariousness of Jordan's morale and the need to relieve him of worry so that he may concentrate on the blowing up of the bridge. Pilar foresees Jordan's death written in his hand but refuses to speak of it (P.p.34, TP.p.36). Later she tells him to forget 'that nonsense of the hand' (P.p.88, TP.p.87) and, after Pablo has deserted them, she says it is 'all gypsy nonsense that I make to give myself an importance . . . I would not have thee worry in the day of battle' (P.p.355, TP.p.340).

Pilar and Jordan recognise in each other the qualities of courage, realism, and compassion which mark the code hero, and which is expressed so often in ironic joking, as when Jordan declares his affection for her and she hides her embarrassment by calling him 'a regular Don Tenorio' (P.p.88, TP.p.87). Her joking is indeed often rougher than that, outspoken, bawdy and coarse. Jordan the college professor appreciates also her graphic description of the attack on the town (Chapter 10) in which pride, shame, guilt and compassionate understanding are so impressively revealed, and her description of her days in Valencia (Chapter 14). Truly she is, in the words of Finito the bull-fighter, 'much woman' (P.p.179, TP.p.171).

Pablo

Pablo's relations with Jordan are also affected by the sub-plot. Suspicious, cunning, fearful, the mere ruin of the leader he once had been, Pablo's resentment of Jordan's presence is complicated by his own lust for Maria. The tension between the two men is increased by Pablo's sly remarks about the snow interfering with Jordan's sleeping arrangements (Chapter 14). But Pablo is a complex character. He is not to be trusted. His treachery includes stealing Jordan's detonators and later shooting the men he had recruited so that he could take their horses for his own people.

'All dead . . . We have plenty of horses now, *Inglés*,' Pablo said P.p.416, TP.p.398).

But he fights well at the guard post, and he is the only one with the skill and leadership to get the guerilla band to safety after the operation.

Structure and style

Hemingway's narrative method, like his prose style, was direct and terse. It was his aim to project people living within the framework of the action of the story, and stripped of unnecessary exterior reference or comment on the part of an all-knowing author. In his novels before *For Whom The Bell Tolls* the unfolding of the story was in strict chronological sequence. The characters were also presented in action, as they would be within the life of the novel: indeed he declared that the business of a novelist is to create living people, not characters. This meant that not only their actions but their conversations must be restricted to the reality of the novel. In a famous passage in *Death in the Afternoon* (Chapter 16) he wrote:

'If the people the writer is making talk of old masters; of music; of modern painting; of letters ; or of science then they should talk of those subjects in the novel. If they do not talk of these subjects and the writer makes them talk of them he is a faker, and if he talks about them himself to show how much he knows then he is showing off.'

In *For Whom The Bell Tolls* he continues to practise what he preaches in this respect. But we should notice that by making one of the people in his novel an educated and highly literate professor turned man of action, he is able to introduce a range of reference to history, politics, literature, and art which enlarges the framework of ideas within which the novel is developed.

There is also an extension of the framework of time within the novel. Although only some seventy hours go by between Jordan's first reconnaissance of the bridge and the last scene in which he waits alone for the pursuing cavalry to come into his line of fire, the time element is enlarged by Jordan's reminiscences of life in Madrid, of his boyhood, and of his grandfather's account of the American Civil War. Further extensions are achieved by having Pilar recount her own memories of her life with the bull-fighter Finito (Chapter 14) and of how Pablo took the town (Chapter 10), and by Maria's account of the shooting of her parents and of her own rape (Chapter 31).

Besides these new devices in the construction of the novel, we should also notice Hemingway's new stylistic experiments. These include the method of conveying the impression of Spanish speech and idiom, usually by giving a Spanish phrase and then repeating it in a rather literal English translation: detailed comment on this is given in the chapter summary notes. So too is comment on Hemingway's attempts to convey the ecstacy of love, in passages of prose-poetry charged with metaphorical imagery and allusion.

In theme, construction, style, and all-pervasive humanity, this remains one of the greatest achievements of a very great novelist.

Part 4

Hints for study

THE MOST USEFUL ADVICE for every student is to get to know the text. It has already been suggested that on a first reading of each chapter students should not spend a lot of time trying to puzzle out difficult phrases and allusions. A swift reading to the end of the chapter should be followed by a more detailed reading in which the notes explaining such difficulties are carefully studied. A further swift reading should then help to establish the contents of the chapter, and its place within the developing structure of the novel, in the student's mind. It should be stressed that, while these Notes provide a valuable guide to the full understanding of the book, nothing can be of greater value to the student than a thorough knowledge of the text itself, which will in turn provide him with the confidence to form his own ideas and opinions about the book and to answer questions on it with freshness and originality.

Throughout the chapter notes and the critical commentary in Part 3 suggestions have been made about both general and particular points to look out for. These concern the theme of the novel, its structure, the literary style, the main plot and the sub-plot, and the characters and their interactions.

Study files

At an early stage in the study of the novel—probably during the detailed chapter reading—many students will find it helpful to start compiling a set of study files in which they can write down notes and key quotations. Always put down after the quotation the page reference to the text you are using: for more general notes, a chapter reference may be sufficient. This will help you to find the passages when you are revising.

Study files should be set up for each character. Amongst the headings on each file you might include (i) physical and character description, (ii) personal history, (iii) role in the action, (iv) views on politics, the war, religion and (v) relationships with other key characters. The compilation of these files should make it easier to answer examination questions both about the individual characters and also about more generalised matters, by bringing together, for instance, contrasting views and opinions, contrasting roles and motivations, and so on.

Sample file: Anselmo

A short specimen file on Anselmo might read as follows (The TP text is used):

(i) 'Short and solid old man' (p.9). Strong: climbs faster than Jordan (p.11). Reliable. Loyal. Unsophisticated—does not distinguish between Division and Staff cars (p.174). Obeys orders dutifully—waits in snow (p.174).

(ii) Peasant from Barco de Avila. Keen hunter (p.41). Now homeless (p.176). Wife dead, no children (p.178).

(iii) Guides Jordan to bridge and camp. Fails to distinguish and report on cars (p.174). Finds bodies of El Sordo's men (p.288). Reports on troop movements. Shoots sentry (p.380)—had not wanted this (p.175). Killed by steel splinter (p.390)—irony, since he had said he would not blow bridge if Jordan on it (p.385).

(iv) 'To me it is a sin to kill a man' (p.43). Bewildered because Republic has abolished God and sin (p.43). War aim—to re-educate his enemies (p.44). Fascist soldiers at guard posts are 'poor men as we are' (p.174). Imagines civic penance for those who have killed (p.177)—i.e. substitutes secular arrangements for religious ones. But prays for El Sordo (p.289). Hopes to atone for death of sentry (p.387)—clearly still deeply religious.

(v) His reliability is a comfort to Jordan (p.181). When they go over plans for the action at the bridge, Jordan's role towards Anselmo is protective, almost fatherly (end of Chapter 14). Observe Jordan's thoughts as he sees Anselmo dead (p.390).

How to use the study files

Cross references should be made to other files, sometimes under special headings. Anselmo's thoughts on killing in war should be cross-referred to Jordan's: 'he told me that he did not mind it' (p.178). See also Jordan's thoughts, (pp.61-2 and pp.268-9): 'no man has a right to take another man's life unless it is to prevent something worse happening to other people'. These cross-references help to show both contrasts in viewpoint and links in the structural components of the novel.

To this outline file on Anselmo more material may be added. For instance, there is another useful quotation about his war aims in Chapter 23: 'That we should win this war and shoot nobody . . . and that those who have fought against us should be educated to see their error' (p.253). Anselmo makes this remark in a discussion with Agustín, who wants to shoot 'the anarchists and Communists and all this *canalla* except the good Republicans'. These quotations can be deployed in answering examination questions as different as:

(1) Write a character study of Anselmo.
(2) Compare and contrast *either* Anselmo and Agustín *or* Pablo and El Sordo.
(3) How far is an understanding of the Spanish Civil War essential to our appreciation of the novel?
(4) Compare Jordan's and Anselmo's moral values.
(5) Discuss why Jordan, the American college professor, and Anselmo, the Spanish peasant, are comrades-in-arms in the operation against the bridge.

Study files for themes, structure and style

Further study files may be built up for thematic or stylistic topics. For instance, a file on how Hemingway presents the development of the love affair between Jordan and Maria would include lists of the imagery in the passages quoted in Chapters 7, 13, 20 and 37 when they make love. In Chapter 7 there are images of smoothness, coolness and warmth (p.68); in Chapters 13 and 37 images of light and darkness, of a passage to infinity, of soaring to a moment when time stops and the earth moves out and away (pp.145 and 334). In Chapter 20 Maria speaks of the sense of fusion: 'I am thee and thou art me and all of one is the other' (p.234). But the file will show that in Chapter 20 there is no passage of metaphorical prose-poetry comparable to those in Chapter 7, 13 and 37. Quotations from the earlier chapters and from the dialogue between Jordan and Maria in Chapter 20 can be deployed in such questions as:

(6) Discuss the development of the relationship between Jordan and Maria.
(7) Hemingway's prose style has been described as declarative and terse. How true is this of *For Whom The Bell Tolls*?
(8) 'Hemingway is a writer of realistic prose whose concepts are those of a romantic poet'. Discuss.

Similar files could be built up for Hemingway's use of irony; for reference to omens of ill luck; for superstitious beliefs; and for hints early in the novel that Jordan is to meet his death. By noting the scenes in which these references are made, and the part they play in the relations between the various characters involved in these scenes, you will get a fuller grasp of the structure of the novel and of the interplay of the actors as the tale develops.

Examination questions

When answering an examination question, read the question carefully to see exactly what the topic is. Organise the points you want to make in the order in which you want to make them. Use quotations from the text to illustrate and support these points. Above all stick to the topic as set in the question. Further specimen questions for revision practice include:

    (9) Discuss the relationship between Pilar and Jordan.

   (10) 'Pilar is the finest piece of characterisation in the novel.' Discuss.

   (11) Compare the characters of Golz, Karkov, and Massart.

   (12) 'An outstanding work of an ideal tendency'. To what extent does the novel measure up to this requirement of the Nobel Literature Prize award?

Specimen answers

Two further examination questions are supplied together with model answers. These show how to present the results of your study of the text and commentary.

---

(13) How successful is Hemingway's attempt to convey the flavour of Spanish speech? Give examples to support your opinion.

When a novelist wishes to portray a foreigner he may be faced with a variety of problems. If the foreigner is to be presented as a comic character these problems are fairly simple to solve. The foreigner's appearance, his dress, his manners, and his speech can be handled as caricatures. A good deal of comedy may be extracted from his speech by making him use the novelist's language—let us say English as in the example of Hemingway—in ludicrous ways, either by translating directly foreign idioms that sound absurd in English, or by making him choose wrong words or expressions so as to suggest comic ambiguities, wrong sense, or even nonsense.

The novelist's problems are much more difficult when, like Hemingway in *For Whom The Bell Tolls*, he is presenting serious characters, not figures of fun. One solution is to ignore their foreignness and make them speak straightforward colloquial English, perhaps with just the addition of foreign polite forms of address, like the frequent use of *monsieur* in French. Hemingway, however, believed that the novelist's task is to make real people talk realistically. Since most of the Spanish characters in the novel are comparatively uneducated peasants, gypsies, and the like, they will have to use the colloquial speech and idioms of uneducated people. To make them use the speech of uneducated English farm workers, dialect words and all, would be unconvincing. A more sophisticated approach to the problem is required.

Hemingway's solution is to put short Spanish phrases or sentences into the mouths of his characters, and then to repeat these phrases or sentences in a fairly literal translation, so that the reader can see what the Spanish means. Early in the novel, for instance, Anselmo says that Pablo 'would like to retire like a *matador de toros*. Like a bull-fighter.' This is a standard English translation. But he also says that Pablo 'is *muy flojo*. He is very flaccid.' This is not standard English but a literal translation. English usage would be 'he has gone soft', but in the context we understand what Anselmo is saying.

If the character is making a longer speech, then the rest is continued in English, but normally with the continuing use of the peculiar style of literal translation. In this way the reader's mind, already attuned to Spanish idiom, is persuaded to accept the whole speech as being characteristically Spanish.

Translation from one language to another may be considered on various levels—vocabulary, grammar and syntax, and idiomatic expression. We find Hemingway operating his device of literal translation on all these levels.

To take vocabulary first, a recurrent example is the use of the word 'rare', from Spanish *raro*, where normal English usage would be 'unusual' or 'strange'. Soon after Jordan arrives at Pablo's camp, Pablo asks for news of the Russian dynamiter Kashkin, 'this foreigner with the rare name', and goes on to say that 'he spoke in a very rare manner'.

A recurrent grammatical usage is 'thou' and 'thee', the Spanish familiar form of the second person singular pronoun, together with the appropriate verb forms. Maria says to Jordan, 'Thou hast loved many others', to which he replies 'Some. But not as thee'. However, Hemingway sometimes mixes these forms with standard English 'you', even in the same bit of dialogue; and while often the speech flows on acceptably, sometimes the switch from one form to the other strikes a discordant note.

Where Hemingway's solution is particularly effective is in dealing with idiomatic expressions, especially with the oaths and blasphemies which so many of the characters use. Examples abound throughout the novel; but there is a striking passage in Chapter 9 where Hemingway actually comments on the formalism of the insults which Agustín and Pilar hurl at each other, e.g. 'I besmirch the milk of thy duty . . . Daughter of the great whore of whores. I befoul myself in the milk of the springtime', and so on.

All in all, one can say that Hemingway reached a very successful solution of the problem. The dialogue put into the mouths of the guerillas does convey, as one critic has put it, 'a skilful impression of the idiom and glorious cursing of Spanish speech, as strongly flavoured as onions and rough wine'.

---

(14) 'In the account of El Sordo's fight on the hilltop Hemingway communicates the essentials of the novel's political and moral themes.' Amplify this statement.

Hemingway's own complex attitude to the politics of the Spanish Civil War can be seen in the way he presents the story of El Sordo's last stand against the Fascist troops. It is not presented as a straight fight between republicans and Fascists, wholly right and wholly wrong. The portrayal of both El Sordo's guerilla band and of the Fascist soldiers is designed to rouse feelings of mixed sympathy for each side.

Hemingway achieves this in a number of ways. He brings into play the attitudes of the two sets of enemies towards each other, the conflicting views within each set, and comparisons between the sets.

El Sordo's men are all committed to the Republican cause. But the older men have a different attitude from Joaquín, the youngster who unthinkingly repeats Communist propaganda slogans. One of El Sordo's men tells Joaquín that La Pasionaria, the Communist leader, is keeping her son safe in Russia instead of letting him risk his life in the war. Joaquín is unwilling to believe this; but the others know full well that on the Republican side, despite all the slogans about equality, the powerful Communists have privileges which are denied to the ordinary citizen. The Left is in this respect as bad as the Right. This theme is illustrated elsewhere in the novel, especially in the passages where Jordan reflects on what he has learnt about politics and power at Gaylord's.

El Sordo, on the other hand, suffers no illusions, least of all about the fact that he is in a fight to the death. He is determined to take with him on 'the Voyage', as he calls it, as many dead Fascists as possible. Yet he has some admiration for his enemies. 'They are brave but stupid people', he thinks; but it is only the stupid slogan-chanting Captain who is tricked when El Sordo pretends that he and his band have shot themselves to avoid capture.

Amongst the Fascists too there are differences, particularly between the Captain and Lieutenant Berrendo. The former is both a bully and a coward, who tries to use his authority to force first a sniper and then Berrendo into walking up the hill. His foul language offends Berrendo and the sniper who are devout Catholics: 'they did not want to have that sort of talk on their consciences on a day in which they might die . . . This one speaks worse than the Reds.' Hemingway stresses these inter-connections again when he makes Joaquín switch from repeating La Pasionaria's slogan to reciting the 'Hail Mary' and a prayer of contrition as the bombs fall on the hillside. It can be argued that in presenting these contrasts on both sides Hemingway is making a point not so much about religion as about the complications of politics and morals in a civil war.

Finally, there is the grim last scene. When Berrendo finds Joaquín unconscious and dying after the bombing, he makes the sign of the cross and shoots him 'quickly and gently'. Then he orders his men to cut off the heads of the guerillas and carry them back to the Army base. 'What a bad thing war is,' he reflects.

The phrase sums up the essential political theme of the novel. In this fight for democracy no one side is absolutely guilty or guiltless, for each side includes individuals of varying degrees of wisdom, courage, compassion, and ruthlessness. By presenting complex contrasts and similarities in the interactions of the individuals who are caught up in El Sordo's fight on the hilltop, Hemingway illustrates to his readers the theme that no man is, politically and morally, an island.

Part 5

Suggestions for further reading

The text

For Whom The Bell Tolls was first published by Charles Scribner's Sons, New York 1940, and Jonathan Cape, London 1941. There are two readily available paperback editions, those of Penguin Books, Harmondsworth, 1955, and Triad/Panther Books, St. Albans, 1976.

Other works by Hemingway

The two major earlier novels, *The Sun Also Rises* and *A Farewell to Arms* will be found to be useful for study purposes.

Criticism

BAKER, CARLOS: *Ernest Hemingway: A Life Story,* Charles Scribner's Sons, New York, 1969. Paperback edition, Penguin Books, Harmondsworth, 1972. The authorised biography.

BURGESS, ANTHONY: *Ernest Hemingway and his world*, Thames and Hudson, London, 1978. A perceptive appraisal illustrated with well chosen photographs.

CARR, RAYMOND: *The Spanish Tragedy*, Weidenfeld and Nicolson, London, 1977. A balanced study of the political background.

SANDERSON, STEWART: *Hemingway*, Writers and Critics series, Oliver and Boyd, Edinburgh, 1961; Grove Press, New York, 1961. Portugese edition, Editorial Presença, Lisbon, 1963; Spanish edition, Epesa, Madrid, 1972; Japanese edition, Shimuzu Kobun Do, Tokyo, 1979. A critical study of Hemingway's work with chapters on his literary technique and on *For Whom The Bell Tolls*.

SANDERSON, STEWART: 'Ernest Hemingway', in Writers of the English Language series, *Novelists and Prose Writers,* ed. James Vinson, Macmillan, London, 1979; St. Martin's Press, New York, 1979. A short introduction to Hemingway's work.

The author of these notes

STEWART SANDERSON served in the RNVR and was educated at the University of Edinburgh, subsequently studying in Italy and Sweden. He was then successively Secretary-Archivist and Senior Research Fellow in the School of Scottish Studies at the University of Edinburgh. He is now Director of the Institute of Dialect and Folk Life Studies at the University of Leeds. He has lectured in many universities in Europe, the United States and various African countries, and in 1974 was Visiting Professor of Folklore and Folk Life in the University of Pennsylvania. His books include *Hemingway* (1961), *The Secret Common-Wealth* (1976), the English Dialect Survey's *Linguistic Atlas of England* (1978) of which he is co-editor, and a forthcoming study of modern urban legends. He has also written many articles on folk life, literature and dialect studies. Elected to corresponding membership of the Royal Gustav Adolfs Academy for Folk Life Research in 1968, he is a Past President and Trustee of the Folklore Society and a Governor of the British Institute of Recorded Sound.